I'VE

GOT

YOUR

BACK

The Indispensable Guide to **STOPPING HARASSMENT** When You See It

I'VE GOT YOUR BACK

Jorge Arteaga & Emily May of Right To Be

Illustrated by Lucila Perini

ABRAMS IMAGE, NEW YORK

We want to dedicate this book to the
thousands of people who have trusted us
with their stories over the past fifteen years.
Your bravery made this book possible.

Contents

INTRODUCTION

For most of us, the desire to intervene in moments of harassment starts with a story.

It might be our own story, when someone treated us as "less than" just for being ourselves. It might have been a slur, an unwanted touch, or that slow-but-steady feeling of social exclusion.

It might be someone else's story. Someone we cared about. Someone whose sense of possibility and belonging was slowly chipped away by the world around them. Someone we didn't know how to help.

Or, we may have unintentionally done some of these things to others—not knowing, or understanding, how it made the other person feel.

Most likely you've experienced all three. And as challenging, confusing, and even traumatic as these experiences may be, they got you to exactly where you need to be. Right here. Welcome.

By picking up this book, you're setting an intention for a different type of world. A world where, yes, harassment may still happen. But when it happens, there will be someone who stands up against it.

It is our deepest hope and desire that that person will be you.

WHAT IS BYSTANDER INTERVENTION?

If I was to have a medical emergency, you'd know what to do. If I dropped my hat on the street, you'd know what to do. But when people experience and witness harassment, they freeze.

Bystander intervention is simply overcoming that "freezing" instinct so we can return to, and act on, that very human desire to take care of one another. It's not about being the hero, strapping on superhero spandex and saving the day. And it certainly isn't about sacrificing your own safety.

There is nothing new or innovative about people taking care of people. And yet it is an exciting reversal in a culture that normalizes violence and isolation.

I've Got Your Back is a culmination of the 500,000+ people we've trained in bystander intervention since 2012 at our organization, Right To Be. Our training and methodology has grown and adapted over time, and in the past few years, we've seen a dramatic surge of interest in bystander intervention. In 2020, we trained six times more people than we did in 2019, and the demand has only grown since then. At the time of this writing, we're training hundreds of people each day in bystander intervention.

Bystander intervention is an idea as old as time. It's the idea that as a community, we've got us.

HOW DO YOU INTERVENE?

This book will teach you how to intervene using Right To Be's methodology, the 5Ds of bystander intervention: Distract, Delegate, Document, Delay, and Direct. Each of these approaches is designed to prioritize the needs of the person being harassed while mitigating risk to yourself.

1. DISTRACT

Creating a distraction to de-escalate the situation.

Distraction draws attention away from the intensity of the harassment and ultimately de-escalates the situation. For example, you could drop your coffee, and people would scramble to help you clean it up or avoid the mess. You could also start a conversation with the person experiencing the harassment. Here, the idea is to build a safe space with the person being harassed while denying the person doing the harassing from getting the attention they are seeking.

2. DELEGATE

Finding someone else to help.

Our favorite potential delegate is the person right next to us. Like us, they could share the very human desire to take care of other people. Unlike us, they probably haven't written this book. Asking them to document a situation, intervene directly, or go and grab the manager while you monitor a situation are simple ways to create support for yourself when intervening, as well as for the person being harassed. You can also reach out to your HR department if you're at work and/or the social media companies where the harassment is occurring—but it's best to check in with the person being harassed first.

3. DOCUMENT

Creating documentation and giving it to the person who was harassed.

Whether you're using your cell phone camera, pen and paper, or saving screenshots and hyperlinks, documentation is powerful. It offers power back to the person being harassed and gives them the reassurance that what happened was wrong—while simultaneously giving them the concrete evidence they will need if they decide to report it.

4. DELAY
Checking in on the person who experienced the harassment.

Sometimes the harassment occurs too quickly for any intervention during the moment, so your intervention happens after the fact, and hence, is delayed. When this happens, a quick check-in can remind the person that what happened wasn't okay and that anyone would be upset by it. When you delay, you're showing them that you've got their back regardless of what they choose to do about it (even if they choose to do nothing).

5. DIRECT
Setting a boundary with the person doing the harassing, and then turning your attention to the person being harassed.

This is the most misunderstood of the 5Ds. It's easy to assume that it's about telling off the person doing the harassing, or at the very least, educating them. But it's not really about them at all—or even about you, for that matter. Like all of the 5Ds, it's about prioritizing the person being harassed. Start by setting a boundary: Say, "Hey, what did you mean by that?" or, "That's so disrespectful; give them some space." Then turn your energy away from the person doing the harassing toward the person being harassed. As tempting as it may be, don't get into a back and forth. People actively harassing others aren't in a mindset to learn at that exact moment anyway.

WHERE DID THE 5DS COME FROM?
Like all good ideas, Right To Be's 5Ds weren't developed in isolation. Inspired by the stories submitted to Right To Be, Emily reached out to an organization named Alteristic (then Green Dot). They had an approach to bystander intervention that was gaining popularity at campuses across the country: the 3Ds. The 3Ds included Direct, Delegate, and Distract.

Emily approached them with the idea of expanding the 3Ds to apply to street harassment. The founder and president, Dorothy J. Edwards, PhD, and her colleague at the time, Jennifer Messina, readily agreed. In 2012, Right To Be launched the "I've Got Your Back" campaign and started training people to intervene. As people began intervening, Right To Be mapped their positive actions on our app with green dots, in a map filled with pink dots indicating harassment.

The work grew from there. Slowly but surely, interest in bystander intervention and demand for our training grew. Along with it, we heard thousands of stories from folks about what worked and what didn't. We iterated our approach as we listened and learned. In 2015, we added "Delay" to expand the 3Ds to 4Ds and in 2017, we added "Document" to complete the 5Ds of bystander intervention, at the recommendation of our partners at WITNESS, an international nonprofit organization that helps people use video and technology to protect and defend human rights. We then expanded the curriculum to address harassment online in 2016, at work in 2018, and then built upon our online harassment work even further in partnership with Viktorya Vilk at PEN America in 2020.

Data shows the training works. In a content analysis of stories submitted to Right To Be before we started training folks in bystander intervention (2005–2011), bystanders had about a 50 percent chance of increasing trauma. Often, this resulted from either bystanders failing to do anything at all—or from bystanders blaming the person who was harassed in the process of intervening (for example, bystanders making comments like, "Oh honey, you know you can't wear that at night if you're going out by yourself").

Now, we've found that 98 percent of people who attend our trainings leave confident there is at least one thing they can do to address harassment the next time they see it, despite most of them having entered the training with significant hesitations.[1] Perhaps even more impressive: Of our attendees who've witnessed harassment since their training with us, 75 percent reported that they intervened.[2]

THIS IS THE MOMENT FOR BYSTANDER INTERVENTION
The rise in interest in bystander intervention comes at a moment of failing trust in the institutions expected to keep us safe. Across the world, we're

watching a dramatic rise in harassment against our most marginalized communities.

This book is filled with stories of harassment—and stories of hope and intervention. As you read through these stories, they may bring up a lot of emotions, and perhaps, memories of your own experiences of harassment. Some may be things that happened yesterday; others you may not have thought about in years. This is normal.

As authors, our intention in sharing these stories is to invite you to face the realities of harassment and to listen deeply to the people impacted by harassment. But we also want to invite you to take care of yourself as you do so. It's okay to take breaks, to pause, to breathe. If you need support processing what comes up for you, skip ahead to Chapter 10, on Resilience.

Whatever may surface for you as you read this book is surfacing for good reason. In the past few years, we've seen spike after spike in incidents of harassment. Here are a few examples from the US alone:

- After the 2016 US presidential election, we saw spikes in hate and harassment in all its forms. On a blog we hosted after the 2016 election to track these stories, one person witnessed a group of men harassing a disabled man by saying he was "a f—ing [slur]" and "only good for making glue." When she approached them to ask why they were harassing the man, they said, "Trump is president, so it's okay."[3]

- The #metoo movement in 2017, led by powerhouse activist Tarana Burke, exposed the cracks in our human resources departments—and institutional willingness to yield to power and money in the face of harassment.

- We continue to see (mostly white) folks perceive Black folks as a threat just for living their lives—resulting in unnecessary calls to the police. For example, in 2018, two Black men were dragged out of Starbucks in handcuffs for "not purchasing anything."

- When COVID-19 hit the US in 2020, we saw a rise in anti-Asian and anti-Asian-American harassment, as people scapegoated those of multiple Asian backgrounds for the coronavirus by calling it the "China virus."[4]

Alongside all this harassment, we've witnessed the failure of our systems: the failure of the criminal justice system to ensure the safety of Black lives; the failure of our health care system to care for the most vulnerable; the failure of our workplaces to ensure the safety of women; and the failure of our schools to safely care for our children.

One of our mentors, scientist and somatic coach LaWanda Yanosik Holland, MBA, PhD, likes to remind us: "After the forest fire, the greenest things grow."[5]

As the metaphorical forest fire rages across the globe and our trust in systems falters, our trust in our own agency and ability to create change is rising. Perhaps for the first time, we see that our actions matter. Or at a minimum, we know our actions are the only thing we can truly control.

Together, we are building a new vision for our communities. One where we stand up for our neighbors, and our neighbors stand up for us. One where we don't have to be perfect to be helpful. One where we know that it's not enough to just claim to be "anti-racist" or "anti-sexist," but that we must actively take steps to undo the culture that made racism, sexism, and all forms of discrimination so prevalent to begin with.

Glossary of Terms

There are some terms we use in this book that you may have never heard of, or never seen used in the way we're using them. We want to take a moment to unpack these terms so that as you're reading, you know exactly what we mean:

PERSON WHO IS EXPERIENCING HARASSMENT: We don't use words like "target," "victim," or "survivor." Here's why: Almost everyone experiences a moment in their life when they are treated as less than, and very few people with whom we've spoken want that moment, however traumatic, to define their whole identity. We also want to restore a person's agency and choice by allowing them to reclaim their own narrative and relationship to the concept of being a victim or target, as these words may not always be how they see themselves in the situation. By calling them a "person who was harassed," we are centering their personhood, their humanity, and intentionally describing what a person *experienced* rather than asserting what a person *is*. This is called "person-first language."[6]

PERSON WHO IS HARASSING: We don't use words like "perpetrator" or "harasser." Just as is the case with people who experience harassment, we don't want to base the entire identity of a person who harasses on a harmful choice they've made. Surely people who harass are also parents and children, artists and athletes, homebodies and go-getters.

By referring to them as a "person who is harassing," we're also taking a step to center their humanity over their actions—with the intention of creating enough space for transformation. We want people who harass others to learn to do better and grow from their mistakes, not forever be locked into them without the chance to do better.

BYSTANDER: A bystander is someone who witnesses harassment. Being a bystander doesn't indicate whether you intervened or not—you can be a bystander who "stands by" and chooses not to intervene, or you can be a bystander who intervenes.

MARGINALIZED COMMUNITIES: Marginalized communities are groups of people who regularly have their needs systemically ignored and/or deprioritized in economic, political, social, and cultural arenas. In this book, some marginalized communities we discuss include communities of color, women, LGBTQ+ folks, people with mental and/or physical disabilities, immigrants, religious minorities, people who self-identify as fat, low-income and poor folks, people who are HIV+, people without housing, formerly incarcerated folks, elderly people, and more. You might notice that these identities are often overlapping—one can be marginalized by societal structures in more than one way.

PRIVILEGE: An unearned set of benefits given to someone based on their race, gender, ability, or other identity. People who hold more privileged ones often have their needs met and/or prioritized in economic, political, social, and cultural activities. And it's often the case that because their needs are prioritized or already met, they often take for granted that these needs are always met in general, not realizing that what they take for granted is a function of privilege rather than equitable access. Examples of folks who hold privilege include white people, cis men, straight folks, able-bodied folks, and others. Most of us hold privilege in some ways and not in others. For example, Jorge has male privilege, and Emily has white privilege, but both are also members of marginalized communities.

CIS: Being cis means that your gender identity aligns with the sex you were assigned at birth. For example, when Emily was born, the nurse said, "It's a girl!" and today she still identifies as female; that makes her a cis woman. You may wonder, "What's the point in saying cis woman, then?" We use this term as a way of being specific when we're talking only about cis women or cis men, because when we use the words "woman" or "man," we mean both cis and trans women and men.

TRANS: Being trans or transgender means you don't identify with the gender that aligns with the sex you were assigned at birth. You may identify as the opposite gender, or you may identify as neither man nor woman—or as both, as multiple genders, as two-spirit if you're Indigenous, as genderqueer, gender-expansive, gender nonconforming, or other genders. Trans is an umbrella term. While some use it to only describe trans men and trans women, we use it to describe all genders that are not cis.

GENDER-EXPANSIVE: Under the umbrella of the word "trans" is gender-expansiveness, or the idea that we are not limited by a gender binary of man and woman. Terms like "gender nonconforming" or "gender diverse" have a similar meaning, but we use the term gender-expansive because we believe it gives us beautiful space to imagine possibilities.

17

THE PROBLEM

WITH

HARASSMENT

Harassment starts young, and it lasts a lifetime.

In school, they call it bullying. In Jorge's case, he was harassed about his weight starting at age six, race starting at age eight, and his sexuality starting at age twelve.

Here's one example from when he was in the third grade: It was the annual school circus, and to celebrate, students got to eat real pizza from the pizzeria instead of the frozen stuff. Jorge grabbed his lunch tray and headed toward the circus in the school gym. As he walked through the door, a group of his classmates waiting just outside the doorway swatted the tray, sending pizza flying all over his face and clothes while screaming, "You don't need to eat that, fat f—k!"

Emily was harassed about her gender and was asked repeatedly throughout middle school if she was a "girl or a boy," mostly thanks to a fabulously short haircut and a flat chest. In high school, it was about sexuality: "Hey, hey, Emily May, how many girls did you f—k today?"

By the time she reached college, it became a stream of endless comments voiced by strange men. Some were whispers: "I want to f—k you in the a—"; some were shouts: "Well, you're ugly anyway!" Sometimes it was silent staring. And *way* too often, it was feeling men standing too close, following too close, or masturbating in the shadows as she waited for the train to arrive.

As a society, we like to pin the problem on just "a few bad seeds." It's an easy sentiment that makes us feel safer. After all, if we can remove the bad actors of the world, we can all be safe. Right? Unfortunately, no.

Harassment is a product of our culture, a culture that despite decades of progress is still racist, sexist, classist, homophobic, transphobic, ableist, xenophobic, and downright hateful.

Culture is a tricky problem to solve because it's inescapable. Uprooting it isn't as simple as just throwing a couple of folks into jail or deplatforming (temporarily or permanently banning) them on social media. We can't "cancel" or shame our way into transforming culture.

This myth of "a few bad seeds" is in part so strong because it lets us imagine ourselves as "the good seeds." It seems to imply that as long as *we aren't* the problem, we're not *part* of the problem. Right? Unfortunately, no again.

In our Bystander Intervention in the Workplace training, we ask attendees in an anonymous survey if they have ever been disrespectful to someone at work. Across our trainings, about 95 percent of people say yes.

As depressing as this statistic may seem on its surface, we actually see it as hopeful—because if 95 percent of people who attend our trainings can admit that they were disrespectful, it means they have the self-awareness to identify their missteps. This is the first step in being able to make a different decision next time.

When we pay attention to the smallest of actions—a single choice, a knowing glance, a kind check-in—we notice our power to change the culture that makes harassment acceptable. To quote one of our favorite activists and thinkers, adrienne maree brown, "Small is good, small is all (the large is a reflection of the small)."[7]

Bystander intervention gives us power in moments of harassment that, for too long, have left us feeling powerless. But before we can intervene, we need to dive in deep to understand the problem we're trying to solve. If we don't understand the problem, its context, and its roots, then our solutions will come up short, too.

Harassment has probably existed since the beginning of time. The old saying, "sticks and stones will break my bones, but words will never hurt me," has nineteenth-century origins. Things like inappropriate staring and unwanted touching were just seen as the "price you pay" for being marginalized in this world. When people complained about harassment, they were perceived as "weak," "thin-skinned," or "hypersensitive." The flaw was understood to be with the person *being* harassed, not with the person harassing.

When we transformed Right To Be from a blog to a nonprofit in 2010, we were denied start-up funding by a major social entrepreneurship foundation who declared in their written feedback that "harassment isn't a significant enough social problem." But the fact that within a single decade, there's been such an emergence of interest in the term "catcalling" (in the past deemed insignificant), tells us otherwise.[8]

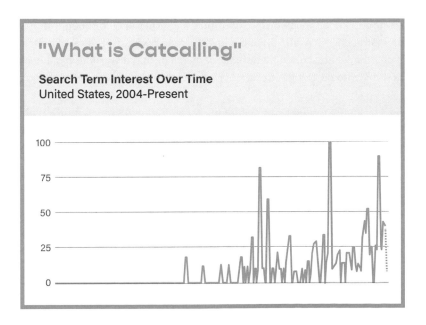

"What is Catcalling"

Search Term Interest Over Time
United States, 2004-Present

How we understand harassment is changing quickly. Dr. Martin Luther King Jr. reminds us that "the arc of the moral universe is long, but it bends toward justice."[9] And we hear the call—it is up to us all (including you, dear reader) to do the bending, even if there are generations more between us and justice.

From the first convention on women's rights in Seneca Falls, New York, in 1848, to the Southern Christian Leadership Conference (SCLC) in Atlanta, Georgia, in 1957, to the creation of the Black Panthers in Oakland, California, in 1966, to the Stonewall riots and the queer rights movement in NYC in 1969, to the Women's March in Washington, D.C., in 2017, we've seen improvement in the material conditions of people experiencing harassment, but we know that there is still work to be done.

As relative newcomers to the party when we started this work in 2005, we dug into the analysis of the activists, researchers, and service providers from generations of feminists and civil rights leaders who understood that normalizing harassment normalizes other forms of violence, too. As we started to speak these truths more broadly, some people thought it was an interesting idea, and on some levels, agreed with us. But most people didn't think harassment mattered *that much,* or that it was *that big a deal,* or that it should be prioritized.

So, like so many who came before us, we shared our stories. Today, Right To Be has collected over 18,000 stories of harassment. We also watched movements like #metoo, #BlackLivesMatter, #StopAAPIHate, and many others that are fueled and refueled by similar stories.

We learned a lot about the problem of harassment. And the more we learned, the more we were able to make the problem visible. We read more stories, heard more conversations, and witnessed more culture change— which looks like more people taking the movement to end harassment in all its forms a lot more seriously.

WHAT IS HARASSMENT, ANYWAY?

If your experience was unwelcome, unwanted, and based in bias, then it was harassment.

Harassment exists on a spectrum of violence. At one end of the spectrum are microaggressions, a term coined by Harvard University psychiatrist Chester M. Pierce in the 1970s to describe the insults and dismissals that

Spectrum of Disrespect

Not listening, speaking over people	Distancing yourself physically or socially from people with marginalized identities	Hateful or biased graffiti or memes
Refusal to acknowledge the contributions of others		Blackface
		Intentionally misgendering people
	Avoiding content/media made by or starring folks from marginalized groups	
Inappropriate staring		Verbal harassment and slurs
Stereotyping		
		Online harassment, including doxxing
Assuming pronouns	Avoiding patronizing businesses owned by marginalized groups	
Assuming gender roles in a couple		Intimidation, such as following someone
	Shaming/humiliation, often in the forms of "jokes"	
Assuming all people from a similar ethnic background look alike		Spitting
	Cultural appropriation	Rape and death threats
Assuming people who hold a specific identity are able to speak for their whole community (e.g., assuming one trans person speaks for all trans people)	Making faces/rolling eyes	Calling 911 to threaten Black folks
	Wolf whistles, animal noises	Inappropriate touching
		Sexual assault
	Intentionally undermining others	Police brutality
Failing to greet or acknowledge certain people		Murder
Microaggressions		

he regularly witnessed non-Black Americans inflicting on Black Americans.[10] Use of the term has since expanded to include behaviors targeted at a wide variety of marginalized groups, including non-Black people of color, LBGTQ+ folks, women, people with disabilities, and others. Behaviors can include things like eye-rolling or people speaking over you—behaviors so common that almost all of us have witnessed them.

As we move along the spectrum of disrespect, we see behaviors more traditionally understood as harassment or hate speech—these include, for instance, comments about people's bodies or racial slurs. And at the extreme end of the spectrum are violent and potentially deadly behaviors like police brutality, abuse, and assault.

We place disrespect and harassment on a spectrum because when you have a culture where speaking over people is acceptable, it enables a culture where shaming/humiliation, often in the form of jokes, becomes a little more acceptable. And when you have a culture where blithe shaming/humiliation is acceptable, it creates a culture where actions that we might traditionally refer to as harassment—such as inappropriate comments, slurs, and/or sexual innuendos—become more acceptable. Normalizing even minor forms of harassment paves the way for even more harmful harassment and/or violence to be acceptable in our culture, too.

IMPLICIT VS. EXPLICIT BIAS

Not all forms of disrespect are based in bias. Things like stress, communication style, and competition can create disrespectful relationship dynamics as well. But bias can be one of many drivers of disrespect, and even more tricky, it can be a driver of disrespect in ways that we may not recognize.

We often think of harassment as a result of explicit bias such as intentional racism, sexism, or heterosexism (discrimination against queer folks). When neo-Nazis walk the streets with torches chanting racist, anti-Semitic slogans, that's explicit bias. But bias is rarely this clear-cut.

Implicit bias, or unconscious bias, is tricky to diagnose and even trickier to uproot. When a white person at a conference lunch is more likely to sit at a table of white people than people of color, but holds no explicit bias towards people of color, that's implicit bias.

Implicit bias often takes the form of harassment that is less obvious to observers and to the person doing the harassing themself, but the experience of harassment rooted in unconsciousness can be equally, if not more, damaging.

Explicit Bias	Implicit (Unconscious) Bias
Expressed Directly	Expressed Indirectly
Aware of Bias	Unaware of Bias
Operates Consciously	Operates Subsconsciously
Example: "I don't like [people from a specific identity]"	Example: Assuming someone of a certain identity lives or grew up in a certain neighborhood

Let's say someone is stressed at work and starts being disrespectful. When people are stressed, our brains look for a "heuristic," or a shortcut in decision-making that is typically derived from comparing the experience in front of you with other mental "prototypes" that you have in mind. For example, "When you are trying to decide if someone is trustworthy, you might compare aspects of the individual to other mental examples you hold. A sweet older woman might remind you of your grandmother, so you might immediately assume that she is kind, gentle, and trustworthy," says journalist Kendra Cherry.[11] While heuristics can create faster, more efficient decision-making, the decisions are more likely to be biased than decisions made when we're not under stress.

SPOILER ALERT:
You have implicit biases.
(Everyone does.)

To effectively mitigate these biases, it helps to know the science behind them. At their best, heuristics are the brain's way of taking care of us. But at their worst, they are rupturing the fabric of our communities, workplaces, and schools.

Fun fact: At any given moment the brain is filtering about eleven million bits of information, but it's only able to pay attention to about forty to fifty.[12]

So how do we filter out the rest? How is it that we can walk down a busy street in New York City with a myriad of stimuli in front of us and still look for a specific person or thing? How can we have a conversation with a friend in a crowd of thousands of people at a rock concert?

Many of us navigate these tasks with something called a "perceptual lens," a mostly unconscious filter that keeps most information out and lets some in, depending upon certain perceptions, interpretations, preferences, and biases that we have adapted throughout our life. The durability and depth of our lens depends on many factors, including neurodiversity—which often affects the ways we process information.

We can experience this in some very mundane ways: If you or your partner were ever pregnant, did you notice how many more pregnant people you began to see all of a sudden? If you were ever looking for a new car, how often did you suddenly start to see that car in commercials and on the street? Our perceptual lens enables us to recognize certain things and miss others, depending on the focus of our unconscious.

Let's consider a different kind of example: Have you ever had a moment when you see something moving out of the corner of your eye and you can feel your body seize in fear?

This is what psychologist Joseph E. LeDoux calls an unconscious "danger detector"—part of our perceptual lens that determines whether or not something or someone is safe before the conscious part of our brain can even begin to make such a determination. That's why we sometimes refer to implicit bias as "unconscious bias."[13]

When our perceptual lens assesses an object, animal, or person as dangerous, a "fight or flight" fear response occurs.[14] On a conscious level, it is possible to correct a mistake by this "danger detector" when we notice it. But often, our brains quickly generate reasons to explain why our danger detector was accurate to begin with, before we can even notice that we might have misread the situation.

We like to believe our decisions are "rational," but in reality, most human decisions are made emotionally on autopilot, and we then collect or generate facts to justify them. When we see something or someone that "feels" dangerous, we have already launched into action subconsciously before we have even started thinking. Our sense of comfort or discomfort has already been engaged. In short, we use our thoughts to rationalize our feelings.

If you hold an identity that someone is biased toward, it means their harassment is likely to be more severe because they are not just stressed—they are stressed *and* biased. Tangibly, this means that while everyone can (and likely has) experienced disrespect at some time or another, marginalized groups tend to experience disrespect more often.

As a bystander, your implicit bias can influence how you choose to intervene. See the table on the next page for examples.

The more aware you are of your biases, the more you can be conscious of your choices about how those biases manifest (or hopefully, don't). Here's the good news: As much as we're wired to exhibit bias, we're also wired to change, grow, and heal to overcome it. It's a concept called "neural plasticity."[15]

Some early research suggests that in the same way we can train our brains to hold bias through repeated exposure to bias, we can also "untrain" our brains from being biased through simple brain experiments. One example is sleep training: A 2015 study showed participants pictures of faces with non-stereotypical words next to them ("female" faces, for instance, had words like "math" beside them) while distinctive sounds were played. When those sounds were played again at an unobtrusive volume during the participants' afternoon naps, the study monitored brain activity and learned that the effects stuck: Participants associated the non-stereotypical words with the pictures more readily.[16]

EXPECT IMPLICIT BIAS, BUT DON'T ACCEPT IT.
Here are some steps you can take to address your own bias:

1. **Build self-awareness.** Watch your mind when you're interacting with others: What makes you tense up? Who do you stand close to? Who do you stand away from? Who do you say thank you to versus who do you just give a tight smile to? Notice if the assessments you're making are a true reflection of you—or product of bias. You can get more information on the biases you hold by taking the free Implicit Association Tests online, developed by Harvard University. There are about fifteen of them available.[17]

Assumptions	How They Influence the Way You Intervene
"Harassment mostly happens in low-income neighborhoods."	You are less likely to be attentive to harassment in other areas.
"People of color are 'loud' and likely to escalate into violence."	You are more likely to create harm for them by assuming danger where there is none.
"Men of color are more likely to harass than white men."	You are less likely to intervene on behalf of people who are harassed by white men.
"People of color are more likely to carry weapons."	You are less likely to adequately assess your safety before intervening in situations where white people are perpetrating violence—and you are more likely to unnecessarily escalate conflicts involving people of color.
"Police presence will make everyone feel safer."	You are more likely to create harm in communities most at risk for police violence, such as communities of color, trans communities, and immigrant communities.
"People from immigrant communities don't speak English."	You are more likely to increase the harm they experience if you try to intervene by speaking overly slowly or loudly to them.
"Some women are just 'too ugly' to be harassed."	You're less likely to intervene on behalf of people you don't find attractive because you're less likely to perceive their experience as harassment.
"People with disabilities are 'childlike.'"	You are less likely to take seriously the concerns and needs they express.

2. **Pause assumptions by asking questions.** Assumptions are shortcuts (heuristics) the brain makes so it can move faster—but it also makes us more prone to mistakes. Instead, when interacting with others, try the "go slow to go fast" approach. Ask yourself, "What assumptions am I making about this person?" And, "Do I know this for sure?" If you don't, lean in with curiosity and ask.

3. **Reduce stress to become present.** The more stressed we are, the more our brain creates shortcuts, makes assumptions, and defaults to bias. Next time you notice your mind spinning, take a moment to clear your mind from everything happening that day, and take a few deep breaths. You may also decide to address stress proactively through regular meditation, exercise, time with friends, or other strategies (check out Chapter 10 for more ideas). Reducing stress can reduce the likelihood that your "danger detector" will mistakenly deploy.

4. **Increase your exposure and listen.** Studies show that being exposed to individuals who contradict widely held stereotypes can override our brains' existing biases. Having friends from different backgrounds can be one component of this work, but be careful not to assume that friends with different identities speak for their entire community. Emily can't speak for all women, just like Jorge can't speak for all men. Instead, read books, listen to podcasts, and listen to the authentic voices of those around you. Make room for the wholeness, and the complexity, of communities—no matter how much you think you know about them.[18]

Addressing bias is a lifelong process, not something that happens overnight. It takes consistent work and deep self-awareness. The most important thing you can do, according to Right To Be trainer and applied theatre practitioner Channie Waites, is to "stay in the game. Don't get frustrated and bench yourself or walk off the field. That's how you get into trouble. You've just got to lean into the discomfort and keep playing."

HARASSMENT AND IDENTITY

Understanding the problem of harassment requires a deep understanding of how people experience the world differently based on identity.

We all hold multiple identities. So when harassment happens, it may not always be clear which identity/identities it's connected to. For example:

Experiencing Public Spaces

What are your identities?
How do they affect how you move through public space?

Have you experienced harassment before?

Do you identify as female or gender-expansive?

Are you a person of color?

Are you from an immigrant family?

Do you have a visual or hearing impairment? Do you have a disability?

Did that person just harass me because I'm a woman? I walk with a limp? I'm unhoused? All three? The question itself may be unanswerable, but the impact is clear: Each marginalized identity that you hold puts you at increased risk of harassment.

For example, women of color are more likely to experience racism than men of color, and trans women of color are more likely to experience racism than cis women of color. For a trans woman of color, what may start off as anti-woman, racist harassment can escalate quickly if the person doing the harassing detects that whoever they are harassing may also be trans

31

or queer. And when marginalized folks are harassed, the harm is more likely to escalate far beyond harassment. In 2020, forty-four trans people were reported killed, the majority of whom were trans women of color, according to the Human Rights Campaign (HRC).[19] The actual number is likely much higher due to chronic underreporting of violence against trans communities—violence that is perpetrated as a direct result of unchecked transphobic bias in action.

To complicate matters further, it's not just the simple layering of identities that defines your experience of harassment. For example, even though all gay men are at risk of experiencing homophobic harassment, their experiences may vary greatly depending on their gender presentation—which could be more masculine, more feminine, gender nonconforming, or even shift from situation to situation. Then, with the further layering of other identities such as race, class, and ability, the experience widens more.

Of course, not all identities are visible, either. While certain physical markers of identity, like your skin color or the fact that you use a wheelchair, may be unavoidably visible, other identities, like your religion or the fact that you live with depression, can be more easily hidden. How visible your identities are is partly determined by how safe you feel making your identities visible to others. For instance, you might not tell homophobic relatives you are a lesbian, or you might choose to share your challenges with mental illness only with people you are confident will understand or relate.

But how visible your identities are may also be a reflection of who is seeing you. For example, in the 1970s, the "hanky code" was a system of color-coded handkerchiefs worn in specific pockets by LGBTQ+ folks to nonverbally indicate sexual interests, preferences, and fetishes. For example, a dark blue hanky indicated an interest in anal sex, and a red hanky indicated an interest in fisting.[20] This allowed LGBTQ+ folks to see each other in a way that was invisible to people who didn't know the code. In this example, an invisible identity was made visible, but only to people perceived as "safe." Once the code became public knowledge, it began to lose its utility (and put LGBTQ+ folks at risk of hate violence). The choice to visibly express your identity for some communities—like LGBTQ+ and religious minorities, for example—can be a careful calculation based on perceptions of safety and belonging.

To complicate matters further, you can be harassed based on assumptions about your identities (even if you don't actually hold those identities). For example, we've received stories from people harassed for being an undocumented immigrant, LGBTQ+, or a woman, who were not actually any of those things. You can also be harassed for being "different," even if the people harassing you can't readily name the difference. This commonly happens to visibly gender-expansive folks, as well as to people whose body movements are considered atypical.

As a bystander, know that everyone's experience of public space will be different and shaped by their identities, whether they be real or perceived. You may not understand *why* someone is being harassed or what kind of bias inspires the harassment, but that's okay. Ultimately, everyone deserves care, so over all else, focus on supporting the person being harmed.

MYTHS ABOUT HARASSMENT

Harassment is so widely experienced—and yet so under-researched. As a result, much of what we *think* we know about harassment is built on myths that are often designed to keep the power structures of our culture (and the act of harassment) firmly in place. In this section, we'll discuss some myths that are especially damaging. Keep in mind, though, this list isn't exhaustive.

MYTH: You can avoid harassment by changing what you wear, where you go, or the time of day you travel.

REALITY: None of these are proven to prevent harassment—but if you ask someone for advice on how to mitigate harassment, chances are you'll hear some of this advice. It's easy to take to heart, because harassment denies you a sense of power and control over how your body is perceived and interacted with. It makes sense that we want to reclaim that power by changing our behavior in hopes of a different outcome. It's hard to feel powerless in the face of trauma.[21]

The problem with these tactics, beyond their inefficacy, is that they mirror the harmful narrative society tells us about harassment: It's your fault. If you did things differently, or if you were different, it wouldn't happen. Try as we might, it's hard to avoid internalizing such messages.

If you experience harassment, it is never your fault. It's not your responsibility to change your behavior; it's other people's responsibility **not** to harass you.

MYTH: The perpetrators of most harassment in public spaces are Black men.

REALITY: There is no credible evidence that Black men are more likely than any other group of people to harass others, or to be more violent in general.[22] However, Black men are much more likely to experience poverty, to have their communities highly policed, to have their faces splashed across the evening news, and to be jailed and/or incarcerated than men of other races.

The idea that Black men have developed a culture that is more tolerant of violence—and more likely to perpetrate it—is a racist myth.[23] If you look around, though, you'll see it repeated over and over again. As long as this myth is left unchallenged, our "solutions" to harassment will be inadequate, continuing to demonize Black men and perpetuate the cycle of violence against them.

MYTH: Microaggressions aren't a form of harassment.

REALITY: While a single microaggression may not rise to the legal standard for harassment, microaggressions can create a hostile work environment.[24]

For example, repeatedly speaking over someone in a work meeting can cause them incredible frustration, especially given that this disproportionately happens to those with less power or authority in the workplace—but outsiders who are used to having their ideas heard and listened to might perceive this as simply "an enthusiastic discussion." By not acknowledging that microaggressions cause harm, outsiders can unintentionally cause the person being harassed to question their own perceptions of reality. This type of action is often referred to as "gaslighting" and can actually deepen the impact of harassment.

No matter where they take place, microaggressions can be exceptionally frustrating to experience, often leaving the person second-guessing themself, asking, "Did they really say that? What did they mean by that? Am I overreacting?" Microaggressions against others are also less likely to be detected by people who haven't experienced them.

MYTH: Companies only care about workplace harassment because they are trying to avoid a public relations scandal.

REALITY: While this may be true for some companies, there are a lot of other viable reasons for companies to care about harassment. Even if you aren't experiencing harassment, knowing it happens can make you feel less safe at work.

Companies with high rates of harassment experience higher employee turnover, lower employee productivity, increased absenteeism, and increased sick leave costs. One study from 2007 found an average damage of $22,500 per employee in lost productivity and employee turnover due to sexual harassment in particular.[25]

A workplace free of harassment is good for both employees and businesses alike.

MYTH: I can say whatever I want; it's my First Amendment right to free speech.

REALITY: While there is space for debate and discussion (as well as conflicting ideas!), what separates harassment from healthy discourse is the focus on harm: threats, slurs, and violence. Harassment limits people's ability to connect and speak freely, regardless of their religion, identity, or political ideology, by conveying to them the message that if they speak their truth, they will be at risk of emotional or physical violence.

KNOW YOUR RIGHTS:
Workplace Harassment Edition

Unlike harassment in public or online, harassment at work has a lot of government regulation at play. These regulations vary from country to country, and inside the United States, they can also vary from state to state.

The following are the federally approved protected classes.[26] This means you can file a complaint with the city, state, and/or federal government if you experience harassment based on:

- Race

- Color

- Sex (including pregnancy, sexual orientation, and gender identity)

- National origin

- Age (forty+)

- Religious bias

- Disability

- Genetic information (including information about an individual or their family's genetic tests and/or medical history)

Some states and cities cover additional forms of bias, including immigration status. To see what classes are considered "protected" in your state or city, use your favorite internet browser to search "protected classes in [STATE or CITY]," check out local laws, or speak with a lawyer.

For each protected class, the US government has different standards for how it defines harassment. There are two types:[27]

- **Quid Pro Quo**—When enduring harassment becomes a condition for employment. For example, a manager or someone else with authority promises a work-related benefit (like a pay raise, promotion, or more favorable schedule) in exchange for a romantic or sexual favor.

- **Hostile Work Environment**— A work environment is considered "hostile" when the harassment is ongoing. At the time of this writing, most states have statutes that the harassment must also be "severe and pervasive," but this is starting to change.

Even if it doesn't rise to a level of what the government may define as harassment, your employer may want to put a stop to these behaviors. Check your employee manual or ask your HR representative how your company defines harassment.

The law supports this analysis and has made harassment illegal in a growing number of contexts. Title VII of the Civil Rights Act of 1964 specifically outlaws sexual harassment in the workplace,[28] and the US Equal Employment Opportunity Commission clearly states, "Harassment does not have to be of a sexual nature . . . and can include offensive remarks about a person's sex. For example, it is illegal to harass a woman by making offensive comments about women in general."[29]

MYTH: There is nothing you can do about harassment.

REALITY: As a bystander, no intervention is too small. Your actions may feel insignificant, but that's rarely the case. The difference it makes may not be immediately obvious, but to the person you're supporting—who has a story of their own with hundreds of different experiences invisible to you—what you do matters.

IMPACTS OF HARASSMENT

If you're reading this book, you probably already know that harassment is not a good thing. But as a bystander, it can be hard to discern how bad it really is.

As a bystander, you're only witnessing a moment. Maybe this time, it *just* looks like a microaggression. *Just* a comment gone sideways. It's easy to think, it wasn't a good thing, but it wasn't *that* bad.

But you can't see someone's full story. And chances are this isn't the first time they have been harassed. In fact, most people we talk to report being harassed so many times throughout their life that they can't count them. If you ask them to guess, they might say, "fifty" or "hundreds," or "I don't know, thousands?" All these incidents build up. They shape us and they change us.

When you intervene in an instance of harassment, you are not just showing up in that one moment. You are really showing up for the other person's entirety of experience, with all that they have been through up to this point right here, right now, with you. You're delivering them hope, a sign that a different culture of care is possible, and that people don't have to go through harassment alone.

Before we move forward and start exploring bystander intervention tactics, let's take a moment to get specific about the impacts of harassment.

1. **Mental health.** Harassment can cause anxiety, depression, and even post-traumatic stress disorder (PTSD).[30] People who experience harassment often report feeling diminished feelings of self-worth and self-confidence.

2. **Social and financial.** Harassment can cause people to change their behaviors and the ways they move through public space. For example, you may start taking a longer route to your bus station to avoid a whole street corner or a whole block where you've been harassed. Or you might decide not to take public transit anymore because you've experienced harassment while using it, so instead you start paying for taxis or you buy a car, both of which are more expensive. If you have a job, harassment can also lead to skipping work—or going to work but not being able to focus because you may be too distressed to focus in an environment where you've been harmed.

3. **Community.** Even when harassment doesn't happen to you, knowing that it happens to others in your community can affect your personal sense of safety. Harassment erodes our collective sense of trust and our overall quality of life.

4. **Public policy.** The way we treat people becomes so normalized over time that it becomes entrenched in policy and law. We have seen countless examples of this: consider the resolution to blame China for COVID-19, the many transphobic bathroom bills, Jim Crow voting laws, redlining, "Stop-and-Frisk," the legalized separation of children from their families at the US/Mexico border, and many more. When we embody hate, it doesn't just leak out of our mouths—it leaks out into our halls of power and becomes the basis for decisions that create even more harm.

Those most marginalized in our society not only experience more harassment, but the harassment is also more severe and thus has deeper psychological, social, and financial impacts. Canadian actor Patrick Kwok-Choon, famous for his role as Gen Rhys on *Star Trek*, reflects on the impact of harassment in his life:

"I have witnessed and been on the receiving end of harassment throughout my life. Unfortunately in most cases, no one intervened to help and it was up to me to confront the harasser in question. Looking back, these attacks were unprovoked violations. Sure, time has passed and scars heal, but the memories are as fresh as the experiences themselves.

For better or worse these experiences have shaped who I am today. I will not put up with injustices when I see them, and a part of me walks around everyday with my guard up expecting that it will only be a matter of time until I face another unprovoked attack."[31]

Even when we are not being actively harassed, the impact of harassment lives in our bodies.

HARASSMENT ISN'T AN UNSOLVABLE PROBLEM

The problem of harassment spans our culture, our thoughts, and our actions. When we start to fully see it, it's hard to unsee. And yet we can't let the sprawling tentacles of the problem of harassment discourage us from finding solutions.

Check out the social-ecological model from the Centers for Disease Control and Prevention (CDC) on page 41.

The individual influences relationships, which influence the community, which influences society. Or said another way, society influences community, which influences relationships, which influence individuals. All of these elements are constantly in conversation. As a member of society, you have influence over all these systems. These systems also have influence over you.[32]

But which is the only one of these systems that you can really fully control? You.

We get stuck when we think of harassment as a large societal problem greater than any one of us. It is a societal problem, of course, but to see it as *only* a problem of society can prevent us as individuals from recognizing and owning our own power.

We can, in fact, through small daily actions, influence relationships, communities, and society. When many of us step into our power and actively model the world that we deserve, culture and systems begin to change.

To end the problem of harassment, we must each commit to the learning and relearning of some core lessons.

- We must practice seeing and holding the full humanity of every person, including ourselves.

- When we cause harm, we must take accountability for our mistakes and learn to go beyond authentic apology to make amends.

- We must commit to learning from our mistakes by repairing harm where possible and forgiving ourselves for the things we cannot change.

- When we experience harm, we must learn to accept authentic apologies and commit to shared transformation.

- And we must find a way to heal ourselves when the apologies that we deserve never come.

While we have often heard the phrase "hurt people hurt people," the inverse is true, too—healing people heal people. When we process the trauma of our own experiences, our healing reverberates—and teaches our relationships, our communities, and eventually our society that healing is possible.

Our acknowledgment and interventions are contagious. When we acknowledge the ways that we, too, have created harm, our honesty and vulnerability reverberates—and teaches those around us, and eventually our society, how to acknowledge. This is the first step in healing the harm that they, too, have created. Likewise, when we intervene on behalf of others, our care acts as a roadmap for each unit of a society to take care of one another, too.

With a problem as big as harassment, it can be hard to step fully into our power and see how our daily actions can change anything at all. But we're not alone. We're part of a global community facing harassment head-on. A global community engaging the right actions at the right time. Together, we're all learning how to use our power, and together, we will tackle this problem in meaningful and profound ways that we've yet to imagine.

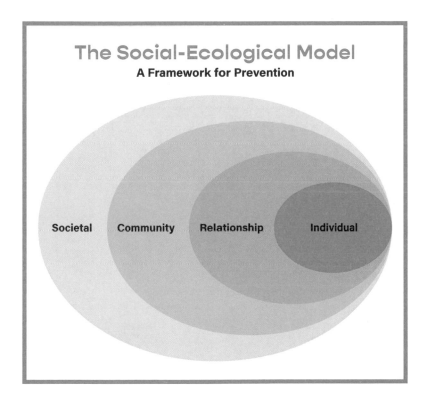

The Social-Ecological Model
A Framework for Prevention

Societal   Community   Relationship   Individual

CHAPTER 3

REASONS
NOT TO
INTERVENE

Before we talk about the productive ways to intervene in a situation, it is worth acknowledging that intervention may not always be the best, or safest, route.

Most people have some concerns about intervening in situations of harassment. This happens for a number of reasons—fear of escalating harm, fear of getting it wrong, fear that our actions won't make a difference. It's normal to worry about these things.

To intervene effectively, we don't want to ignore these concerns, or even "overcome" them. Instead, we want to hold them as true. These concerns are our bodies' and minds' ways of taking care of us and protecting us from potentially harmful situations. Our instincts—or those "flight or fight" modes we experience—are worth paying close attention to.

Our concerns are unique to each of us and can vary based on the situation. Our personalities, identities, and trauma histories can shape how we perceive situations of harassment. So can the environment we're in, who else we are around, and the events unfolding.

Just like our judgments, our concerns about intervening are influenced by our beliefs, perspectives, and personal interpretations. So while we should hold them as valid, we should also be aware that they may not always be accurate. Our biases may distort our perception.

This is why, as we discussed in Chapter 2, it's so important to do the internal work to unlearn our implicit biases. That work happens outside of the moments of harassment in which we intervene—it's lifelong learning and preparation for us to know when and how to intervene most helpfully. And in the moments when we do intervene, it's important that we acknowledge the full humanity of those involved in the situation—understanding the relationship between our concerns and our biases is our key to doing that.

By identifying our concerns about intervening, we can find ways to move into action to help someone experiencing harassment, while still holding those concerns as valid and ensuring our own safety. Once we've identified what exactly makes us feel uneasy about intervening in a situation, we can then use it to help us choose what would be our best form of intervention at that moment.

Our concerns should never be used to determine whether or not we want to help someone—but rather to determine *how* we can help them while ensuring our own safety. Regardless of what our concerns are, in almost all cases there is at least one thing we can do.

Is This a Concern . . .	in Public Spaces?	Online?	at Work?
I'm concerned for my safety.			
I don't know what to do.			
I'm afraid it's going to turn on me because of how I look/ sound/appear/identify.			
I'm afraid it's going to escalate into police violence.			
I'm afraid I'll make things worse.			
I don't have enough context for what's going on.			
I'm worried about looking like a white or male savior.			
No one else is doing anything.			
Other:			
Other:			

ACTIVITY: MY COMMON CONCERNS LIST

In this activity, we are going to build our own list of concerns. On the opposite page, you'll find a checklist with common responses from our training attendees on what concerns them about intervening in public spaces, online, or in the workplace.

Once you've created your own list of concerns, you can choose either to read this chapter straight through or to jump around in this chapter to each of your personal concerns. Following each concern, you can read more about what it means to hold it as valid, and what strategies for bystander intervention might work for you in a situation where this concern comes up for you.

Take a moment to fill out the chart on page 44 to identify which concerns you're holding.

Now that you've created your list, you are ready to read on about what you can do to address your concerns and still be an active bystander intervening to support people in your community.

It is possible that you are holding a concern that is not listed here. We've shared the responses that we most commonly receive, but we realize these are by no means the only concerns one can hold. If you have concerns not listed here, we encourage you to write them down in the list above and share them with us via social media. We will respond and share other options for intervention that might work for you!

I'M CONCERNED FOR MY SAFETY.

Your safety is the number one priority.

If you've ever been on an airplane, you might remember that airlines' safety protocol videos encourage you to put your own oxygen mask on before helping others. The same rule applies to bystander intervention. Ensuring that we feel safe ourselves allows us to be fully present in the situation and fully focused on taking care of the person being harassed.

We often think of intervening only in the most extreme forms of harassment or violence. We assume that there is only one way to intervene, by inserting ourselves into the situation directly. But there are subtler ways of intervening. As we'll unpack later, four of the 5Ds of bystander intervention are actually indirect forms of intervention.

However, the people most likely to recognize harassment and thus intervene—perhaps because they've been a target themselves—tend to be the people also at greatest risk of the harassment then turning toward them.

If you're going to step into a situation, it's important to acknowledge the specific context of the forum in which the harassment is taking place. Here are three of the most common places we may witness harassment:

In public spaces, our safety concerns may be related to multiple factors, like time of day or number of other bystanders. We might fear that the person harassing could escalate into violence or have a weapon.

Online, safety concerns are pervasive, because as interveners, we can never know the motives or extent of further harassment that may unfold in a semi-anonymous forum. Moreover, many who harass online use tactics like targeting people who come to the defense of those they were originally harassing.

At work, our safety concerns are layered. We can be concerned about the economic security threat of losing our jobs, the emotional security threat of

In the case of workplace harassment, you may be worried about retaliation from your boss or coworkers if you intervene in harassment. Retaliation is when an employee is treated differently or loses privileges/responsibilities as a result of intervening in a situation of harassment, reporting harassment, filing a complaint, testifying on behalf of someone else who reported discrimination, or assisting in an investigation. You are protected from retaliation by US law.[33] To learn more, review your organization's policies around retaliation and whistleblowing. It is important for us to understand what recourse we may take in the event that a manager or supervisor retaliates against us for standing up for a colleague.

enduring retaliation or a hostile work environment, or the physical security threat of danger or escalation. Our safety concerns may extend beyond ourselves. For example, you may worry that by intervening you may put your coworkers in jeopardy by drawing attention to the issue.

If you're concerned for your safety, there are ways you can take action. You can find someone else to help you (Delegate). You can also check in with someone who was harassed after the fact (Delay) or create a paper trail of the abuse (Document). If you witness harassment online, you can preemptively tighten your digital security using our guidelines in Chapter 9, and if it's in the workplace, you can read up on internal policies for reporting abuse before you decide to report. When you do report, you might bring a friend (Delegate). These indirect approaches to bystander intervention can help us be effective bystanders while still holding our concerns about safety as true.

I DON'T KNOW WHAT TO DO.
You're not alone. Many people experience a moment where they witness harassment and want to do something, but instead they end up freezing.

There are valid reasons for this: Maybe you have been fortunate enough to have never experienced harassment or harm before. Maybe you have negative associations with conflict, or believe that the only way to intervene is *very dramatically*, like in the movies. Maybe you have been taught to "mind your own business" for fear of violence.

For example, Jorge grew up in Bushwick, Brooklyn, before it was the hip and artsy place it is now. Bushwick before the 2010s was notorious for gang violence, guns, drugs, and trash-filled empty lots. It was not a neighborhood you ventured alone unless you were going to parts where people knew you or your family lived.

Jorge grew up watching the women in his family stand up for others when they witnessed injustice or abuse. Yet, at the same time, they also often advised the young members of the family to mind their business when in the streets, and they would often tell Jorge, *"No te meta en lo que no te importa,"* or "Don't get into what's none of your business."

This was confusing. It led Jorge to believe that there was something he hadn't learned about standing up for others, or that he simply didn't have the strength of character to do so. Whenever he was confronted with the sight of someone experiencing harassment, he would freeze. Unsure of what to do, he was stuck between two feelings: "I don't know how to help these people" and "I don't have what it takes to help them."

Since he'd been instructed to mind his business, he had never helped anyone, and the only examples of interventions he'd seen were all direct, confrontational, and sometimes violent, Jorge was conflicted. As he began to make sense of this over the years, he realized that his family's advice came from their experience of being from a community of color, where the police weren't automatically called in situations of harm—because they were not trusted, and folks didn't feel like they would receive justice or help. This advice also came from a place of only knowing how to intervene by directly getting involved and saying something—helping others but putting yourself in harm's way while doing so.

Over the years, Jorge learned that this was not the only way to help someone. He learned that intervening did not have to mean getting physically involved, fighting, or cursing, but that intervening meant truly showing support to the person experiencing harm by doing simple acts like checking in or finding someone to help.

Whatever your reason may be for not knowing what to do, you've taken the first step toward addressing it by reading this book. Once you've finished, you will walk away with up to five different things you can confidently do to intervene in harassment, and even teach others to do. And they don't require you to put yourself in harm's way.

Here are some ways this concern may arise for us when we witness harassment:

In public, it could be late at night and there may not be anyone else present. Or we may be in a crowded space like public transportation or a bar, and we may not know the first step to take. We might be watching a situation unfold and have a million ideas for how to intervene—but all of them just seem . . . well, bad. We want to ask the person being harassed what they want us to do, but we can't.

Online, harassment has existed since the early days of the internet, and yet it is still far more complicated than it should be to report abuse or utilize digital safety tools to blunt the impact of online harassment. The internet— with its apps, platforms, and specific culture—is constantly evolving and changing, and it can feel like we need to get a PhD in computer science to make sense of any of it.

At work, there are organizational policies, HR departments, and laws to navigate and/or report workplace harassment. While it's very significant that this infrastructure is in place to begin with (as a result of some hard-fought feminist and activist battles), it can be deeply complicated and obscure to navigate. If it leaves you wondering "was this designed to protect the employees or the company?"—you're not the only one. Too many of us feel as though we have very limited options. We fear potential retaliation if we intervene. We need the economic security of our jobs. We resign ourselves to believing that disrespect and/or harassment at work are just conditions we must face to have a job.[34]

Not knowing what to do can leave us feeling afraid, stuck, hopeless, or simply overwhelmed. It is important and brave to acknowledge such emotions as they come up. By acknowledging that we do not know what to do, we welcome the opportunity to learn. In some ways, we also ensure the safety of ourselves and others, because trying to intervene without knowing how to do it could lead to escalating a situation, making it worse, and creating an unsafe environment for ourselves and the person(s) experiencing the harassment.

But we can still take action.

If "I don't know what to do" is one of your concerns, we've got five strategies for you—so keep reading! Here's a place to start: Ask for help from someone else who may know what to do (Delegate). If getting help is not an option, you could check in with the person who experienced the harassment after the situation is over to make sure they're okay and to ask how else you can support them (Delay).

I'M AFRAID THE HARASSMENT IS GOING TO TURN ON ME BECAUSE OF HOW I APPEAR OR IDENTIFY.

Earlier we discussed how our identities as a bystander may affect how we perceive what's happening, how we are perceived by others, and how we choose to show up to support others. As a bystander, your identities can directly impact your safety.

If you hold identities that are historically marginalized, then there is a higher likelihood that the harassment in which you're trying to intervene will turn on you. This is especially true if you share any number of marginalized identities with the person being harassed.

For example, let's say you witness a Black person with a disability being harassed, and you yourself are also Black and disabled. The only thing you know about the person doing the harassing is that their behavior is racist, ableist, and causing harm to someone who has a lot in common with you—so of course it's valid to be concerned for your own safety! Remember: As we said earlier, your safety is the number one priority.

In public, the prevalence of bias in our society can prevent people who hold marginalized identities from intervening, due to the risk that they will wrongly be identified as the person doing the harm—by the person being harassed, by other bystanders, or by the police.

For example, a concern commonly brought up by men is that they are afraid to approach a situation where another man is harassing a woman—because they are worried the woman might think they are going to join in the harassment. For men of color, particularly Black men, this is exacerbated, as they have been stereotyped and framed as sexually pred-atory to white women in white-dominated places throughout history. In the US, this stereotype has existed since white colonizers began kidnap-ping and enslaving Africans in the early 1600s, but it was solidified even more in the Jim Crow era in the 1800s—and it still exists to this day.[35]

Online, it's normal to worry that the harassment may turn on you if you intervene, and the severity and impact of the harassment may increase if you hold marginalized identities. Although it may be easier to obscure your specific identities online—photos and avatars may not reveal that you're neurodiverse, queer, an immigrant, a religious minority, or trans—the risk of being harassed if you stand up for someone else still exists. Moreover, if for safety reasons you're intentionally hiding any parts of your identity from an employer or your parents, for example, online harassment and the attention that can come with it may mean that you risk exposure.

In the workplace, we may fear being labeled the "overly sensitive person of color" on the team if we intervene to support someone. Or we may worry that others will perceive us as exaggerating or taking someone else's experience too personally. Even worse, we might be told things like "no one on the team would ever behave that way," or that we did not in fact witness what we're saying we did (such statements are examples of gaslighting).

Beyond safety concerns, witnessing harassment—especially witnessing a form of harassment to which you are also vulnerable—can be deeply trau-matizing. When you feel angry, triggered, despondent, or you find yourself disassociating by putting on your headphones or turning the other cheek—watch these emotions and responses emerge. Try not to judge yourself for having them. This, too, is taking care of yourself. Instead, take a breath. Try to consider what other ways you might be able to help the person experi-encing harassment. If you don't feel that intervening directly is a physically or emotionally safe option for you, consider Distract, Document, Delegate, or Delay instead.

I'M AFRAID IT'S GOING TO ESCALATE INTO POLICE VIOLENCE. Being arrested is a major concern especially for marginalized groups, not only because of the impact of arrest itself, but because of the likelihood of police involvement escalating into violence. Historically, more privileged people and institutions—including and especially law enforcement—have tended to immediately categorize these marginalized groups as a "threat," and such bias has deadly impacts on these communities.

In public, men of color who intervene, especially Black men, are at increased risk if police are present. For example, in October 2020, Jonathan Price, a thirty-one-year-old Black man, was shot by police after intervening to de-escalate a dispute between a man and a woman at a gas station in Texas. NBC reported Price was "known as a hometown hero, a motivational speaker, a personal trainer, an athlete, a community advocate and a mentor who worked with children."[36] He was clearly a great person, but Black people don't *need* to be exceptionally great to deserve to live a life free from police violence. The risk of police presence to Black folks is very real, whether they are involved in a situation, intervening in one to de-escalate conflict, or just happen to be present but uninvolved.

Online, the police also use virtual forums to self-organize and perpetuate hate. For example, Facebook contains numerous groups and pages where police post racist, misogynistic, homophobic, transphobic, and xenophobic memes and language.[37]

The police also use social media to track civilian activity. During the Black Lives Matter protests of 2020, police deployed a controversial artificial intelligence startup, Dataminr, to help them digitally monitor the protests and individual protesters.[38] This kind of behavior isn't new. In 2004, Emily hosted a fundraiser called "RNC [Republican National Convention] Not Welcome" in her Bushwick, Brooklyn home. The event was advertised on social media only—and was almost instantly infiltrated by plainclothes cops, whom she saw standing in the corner, drinking water.

At work, it may seem ridiculous to call the cops on your coworkers or have the cops called on you while at work—but it still happens. At one New

England university, a Black man headed into work one day when his office was closed, only to have the police called on him.[39] He was interrogated by police and treated as if he had done something wrong. It wasn't until the police figured out he was an employee there that they disclosed to him a member of the campus community had called 911 to report an "African American, bald, red/white pinstripe shirt, dark khakis, large duffle bag on the right shoulder, hanging off a strap, very heavy hanging on the ground, seemed very agitated." In some cases, Black people have even had their own coworkers call the police on them.

People with privilege have deployed the police against marginalized people as a way to wield power against them. This is never okay, and it is never your fault if you are a Black person and this is done to you. Because it's never your fault, it's also not on you to change your behavior. Police encounters put Black people at risk due to police bias, not due to the behavior of Black folks.

To non-Black folks—especially white folks reading this—seeing police presence offers a key opportunity for your to intervene and reduce the likelihood of police-sponsored violence because you are less likely to be targeted by it. Keep in mind the laws and regulations around interacting with police: Try to keep a safe distance, avoid becoming confrontational, and do not interfere with police or with an arrest while it is taking place. Comply with officers' commands to step back or be quiet, and do not strike, throw things at, or make physical contact with the police. You should know that without probable cause, it is illegal in most jurisdictions for police officers to detain, arrest, or search you. You can learn more about your rights when engaging with police in Chapter 7, Document.

I'M AFRAID I'LL MAKE THINGS WORSE.

This is a common concern, especially among people who assume that direct intervention is the only way to respond to harassment. In the movies, we often see people heroically intervene directly. They show up, say the perfect thing to shut the harassment down, or maybe throw a punch at the person harassing. As satisfying as it is to see this happen on the big screen, we all know these strategies don't work so well in real life. There is no "perfect thing" to say, and violence more often than not escalates to further violence.

This concern is especially important if we're dealing with someone who is agitated, irritable, or angry, and we don't want to intervene in a way that might set them off and cause them to escalate. Or, in a situation where the parties harassing and being harassed know each other (such as in a domestic dispute, for instance, or a child/parent relationship), we may worry that if we intervene, the person being harassed may experience some form of retaliation later.

In public, when surrounded by strangers, we can lack context to know how our actions will be perceived. We may wonder, "Do I remind that person of their best friend or their worst enemy? Are they potentially biased against my identities?" These factors may influence others' responses to our intervention.

Online, we may not want to fuel the flames of harassment. We wonder, "By chiming in, even if my comment is supportive, am I bringing more attention to the harassment? How does my action impact the algorithm? If more people see the harassment going on—will they speak out against it? Or will it silence them?"

At work, we may worry that our intervention puts the person we are trying to help at risk of losing their job—or we may worry that by bringing attention to the harassment, we may cause some level of social isolation for them. When we see harassment happening at work, it's unfortunately not uncommon to seek out "reasons" or "justifications" for our coworker's harassment. The logic goes something like this: If the harassment is truly random, it means we are all at risk, but if we can imagine a "reason for the harassment" that we believe would "never apply to us" we can imagine that we are safe from harassment. Practically speaking, this can create an environment where the person being harassed is ostracized—especially when the "reason" that others imagine is related to their clothing or self-presentation, their work performance, their personal life, their habits, etc.

The process of sensemaking by colleagues, self-protective as it may be, can dramatically deepen the harm to the person being harassed.[40]

In such situations, it's better to err on the side of caution and utilize an indirect form of intervention. Some strategies include distracting from an uncomfortable topic of conversation, reporting a thread of comments in the virtual workspace, or checking in with the person on the receiving end of the harassment. If you witness the harassment at work in person, try to make eye contact with the person being harassed, to indicate nonverbally that you recognize what's happening and want to help.

I DON'T HAVE ENOUGH CONTEXT FOR WHAT'S GOING ON.

When we don't have enough context in a situation, we worry about getting it wrong. But take comfort in this: None of the forms of bystander intervention that we teach you are designed to create additional harm for the person being harassed. In fact, many people report feeling supported by a bystander who intervened, even in situations where they weren't actually being harassed.

In public, it's rare to feel like we have enough context for what's going on. We wonder, "Why is this happening? Who are those people? Has someone already been called?"

Online, there is often context to be found if we search hard enough, but is it accurate? The internet is so fraught with misinformation that it's hard to know what is true and what isn't.

At work, it can feel like all the context is hidden behind closed doors. For example, we might wonder, "Is that person's boss reprimanding her for doing a bad job, or because she's trans and the boss is transphobic? Has someone already reported this issue to HR?"

Our advice is this: Instead of focusing on the details of the harm, focus on the impact. Is the person being harassed uncomfortable or distressed in any way? If so, it's a good idea to find a way to intervene and support them.

This can be achieved with any of the 5Ds—even Direct, though it might not seem obvious how. One form of direct intervention is to ask clarifying questions like, "What did you mean by that comment?" or, "Why did you get so close to them?" This can sometimes help you gain clarity on what is happening or whether it's harassment, without potentially escalating a situation by making someone feel as though you're accusing them of something.

I'M WORRIED ABOUT LOOKING LIKE A WHITE OR MALE SAVIOR. A tricky aspect of bystander intervention is that if we're not self-aware, we can draw out the part of us that wants to "save the day" or "save" others.

Bystander intervention isn't about heroics. But even more to the point, it isn't about you as the bystander. The more privileged we are, the more we have probably been influenced, consciously or subconsciously, by the pervasive idea that people with more marginalized identities than ours are too weak or vulnerable to take care of themselves. Our privileges, along with implicit biases, may even lead us to think folks with less privilege don't know what they need—or that they need to be "told" what they need. Such beliefs may not be conscious, but they are widespread.

If you're in a position of privilege while intervening in a situation of harassment and appearing as a "white savior" or a "male savior" is a concern that comes up in your mind, that's actually great news. Why? Because being *aware* of this dynamic is the first step toward making the most helpful, informed choice you can. Recognize your concern so that you can see if and when it interferes in your attempts to help another person.

In public, our privileges—to the extent that they are perceptible by others—may mean we are perceived as untrustworthy, or even dangerous, by those who don't share the same privileges. For example, LGBTQ+ folks may be less trusting of straight women who claim to be allies to the community because of their direct experience with these women entering LGBTQ+ spaces, taking up lots of space, and being disrespectful to LGBTQ+ patrons and performers. Miz Cracker, a well-known drag queen, wrote in *Slate*, "[Straight women] declare their allegiance to queers, they make jokes based on outmoded perceptions of queer life—but most of all they make a lot of tone-deaf noise that can entirely ruin the night for a room full of queer patrons."[41] While these women's intention may be to show allyship, their impact is, at best, to ruin the spirit of the evening—and at worst to harass the very people they claim to support. Successful intervention depends on building genuine trust, and it's more serious work than just being around a community.

Online, where we are mostly reduced to avatars, having privilege often means we are less likely to be trolled. It also means that if we intervene, we'll likely get more praise and accolades for our intervention than less privileged folks will for theirs. Even if our intentions are good and we aren't trying to center ourselves, this can have the effect of pulling attention away from the person being harassed and/or from the other bystanders intervening to support them. If this happens to you, take care to redirect the attention. For example, "the real hero here is [the name of the person who was harassed] for having to put up with this all the time!"

At work, our coworkers have more exposure to us and are likely to know more about us than just the visible privileges we hold. This can support trust-building with the folks with whom we're allying, but it's also import-ant to be thoughtful about how others perceive us and our actions. We have to work hard to prevent narratives that perpetuate the idea of those of us with more privilege as "heroes" and those of us with less privilege as "weak and/or vulnerable."

Intentions can't solve everything; they aren't magic. But they are relevant. If our intention is to make the person being harassed feel safe and sup-ported, that will shine through (most of the time). However, if our focus as a bystander is on ourselves, i.e., "*I'm* going to say something," "*I* can fix this," or "*I* can handle this," then we're not centering the person being harassed. And although it may not be our intention to create additional harm, such a mindset can have that impact. Treating marginalized folks as people who need "saving" can cause them to second-guess themselves and their own inherent strength. It can also lead to them picking up on this "savior mindset" and feeling uncomfortable or wary around those of us who espouse it. After all, historically, the "savior mindset" has not been good for folks with less privilege on a global scale, as countries like Great Britain and the United States have used it—and unfortunately continue to do so—as a justification for invading and/or colonizing other countries, creating tremendous harm.

As bystanders, our goal is to restore a sense of agency for the person being harassed in the situation. If we're able to, we should check in with them and ask them what we can do to help (Delay). If someone being harassed is already standing up for themselves, then rather than trying to interject, we should stand in solidarity with them and support them by being present so they know someone else has their back. We may also choose to Delegate the act of intervening to someone who may have more context for the situation and be able to build trust more quickly with the person being harassed. When taking this route, however, be sure to stick around to support that person, and offer to Document the harassment.

NO ONE ELSE IS DOING ANYTHING.

This kind of thinking is called the "bystander effect." It's a term coined by Bibb Latané, a social psychologist who has done significant research on bystander intervention.

In 1968, Latané, alongside his colleague John Darley, did a series of studies on how the number of people in a room influenced how long it took a study participant to help another person in an emergency. In one study, Latané and Darley placed subjects in one of three conditions: alone in a room, in a room with two other participants, or in a room with two people who were in on the experiment but pretended to be other unsuspecting participants. As the participants sat filling out questionnaires, smoke began to fill the room.[42]

Of the participants who were alone, 75 percent reported the smoke to the experimenters before the experiment was finished. In contrast, just 38 percent of three person groups assembled by Latané and Darley reported the smoke. In the final group, the two people who were in on the experiment noticed the smoke and then ignored it—and of the actual study subjects in that room, only one person of the ten reported the smoke.

Smoke is visible, obvious, and universally agreed upon as a threat of danger. Now, imagine that instead of seeing smoke, the participants witnessed harassment. Harassment is complicated, subject to interpretation, and despite our best efforts, it's still not universally accepted as "bad."

In another study, Latané did the same test, this time with a woman in distress instead of smoke filling a room. The study showed that 70 percent of people would help the woman when they were the only witness, but only about 40 percent offered assistance when other people were also present. Latané and Darley identified a number of potential explanations for this "bystander effect," but the challenge to the movement against harassment is ultimately to overcome that effect—to encourage people to intervene regardless of whether they're the sole witness or in a crowd of hundreds.

In public, it's easy for responsibility to become diffused. The more people are there, the more quickly it happens. Usually, the first person to take action does something really small, like simply asking "What's going on here?" or exclaiming "Whoa, whoa, whoa!" This small action inspires others to notice, step up, and take action, too.

Online, the diffusion of responsibility happens at a mass scale. A single moment of harassment can be witnessed by millions—and yet none might respond or offer support to the person being harassed, leaving that person feeling deeply alone.

At work, if no one else intervenes, we may worry about eroding relationships and being perceived as a "troublemaker" who is always intervening. And yet, speaking up for colleagues demonstrates that we value and respect them, and it helps create a sense of camaraderie, belonging, and ultimately trust within a team.

Small actions that interrupt harassment or disrespect send a message to others that the behavior is not tolerated. Such actions also make the person experiencing the harassment or disrespect feel like someone has their back. We want to disrupt the cycle that allows a whole crowd to stand by and wait for someone else to act. It can feel intimidating to be the first person to say or do something, but one small initial action is often all it takes to motivate others to join you in intervening. And getting others to help out—as you'll see later on in this book—is itself an effective way to intervene.

HERE ARE SOME THINGS TO DO BEFORE INTERVENING:

1. **Always prioritize your own safety.** Seriously, your safety matters. You matter. Before you start intervening in harassment, remember these three steps. If you're in a public space, notice your surroundings, the situation, and what's happening around you. Then consider what is bringing you pause and what concerns you are holding. Recognize them as valid. Last, based on your assessment, decide which of the 5Ds is the best option for you. Before intervening online, take steps to tighten your own digital security (check out the resources in this book's Resources for more information on how to do this). And at work, make sure to check your organization's policies around reporting harassment or discrimination. Prepare yourself for a potential investigation if you choose to report.

2. **Check in with the people targeted by abuse whenever possible.** Harassment can be scary and often makes people feel vulnerable and unsafe—so as a bystander, work to create a safe space around them however possible. Help restore their choice and agency by supporting them, whatever way they may choose, to respond to the harm. Online abuse is disempowering, but checking in with quick chats, DMs (direct messages), and emails is easy. Give them their power back by simply asking what kind of support they would like. And at work, while checking in with people builds a culture of respect and empathy, it also lets the rest of the team know that you have their back and that you do not tolerate disrespect.

3. **Never abuse the abusers.** It can be tempting, but it's never a good idea. It's unlikely you will get through to them with an impassioned explanation of why their behavior is wrong. It's much likelier they will escalate their harassment into worse harm if you engage with them beyond the bare minimum. Bystander intervention is first and foremost about prioritizing the person being harassed and breaking the cycle of abuse.

Whatever your concerns are, hold them as valid. They are designed to protect you and keep you safe. Then, decide how you want to intervene.

Ready to learn how? You got this.

WHAT KIND OF BYSTANDER ARE YOU?

No one has the responsibility to do everything, but everyone has the responsibility to do something.

A major part of being able to move into action is learning which of Right To Be's 5Ds of bystander intervention feels the most comfortable for you, based on the type of harassment you're witnessing.

In the next few pages is a quiz designed to help you identify which of the 5Ds is your Superpower, or the leading tactic you're most likely to use when you witness harassment. Each scenario will highlight a different type of harassment across public, online, and professional spaces. Review each closely, reflect on what response feels right, and choose the intervention option(s) you find most relatable for each scenario. Before you choose an answer for each of the scenarios, reflect on your identity as a bystander and your initial gut reaction to what is happening. Then, as in the previous chapter, take time to write in your concerns about intervening. Do you have one or multiple? Sit with them. Once you've assessed your concerns, consider what your response to the situation could be.

As we learn more about our intervention styles, pay close attention to which scenarios lend themselves to easy intervention and which feel a bit more difficult. For situations that may feel more difficult, it's important to reflect on what makes you feel uneasy. Each scenario allows space to process your concerns, which we hope will support you in understanding what may be bringing you pause in a situation. We encourage you to be honest with yourself and think about what concerns you might be holding in each scenario. This is designed to encourage you to reflect on how you can best show up to support people while still taking care of yourself and listening to your instincts.

There are no right or wrong answers. This quiz is designed to help you understand yourself a little better, not to limit you to a single intervention or set of actions. Once you've completed the quiz, tally up your responses and turn to the resources section to find out which of the 5Ds is your Superpower. We also encourage you to look at your second, third, fourth, and fifth ranking strategies to learn more about other tactics.

CONTENT WARNING: Before you begin, we'd like to note that the situations presented may be graphic or triggering. While we encourage you to complete the entire quiz, it's okay to take breaks. Feel free to set the book down, take some deep breaths, take care of yourself however you need to, and come back to us when you're ready.

1 You are at the deli, waiting for a sandwich. You notice a Black patron come in, purchase a drink, and leave. When the transaction is over, the store clerk that sold him the drink leaves, and a different one emerges from the back room.

The patron stands out front to rest and takes a sip of his drink, and at that very moment the store clerk who just emerged goes outside and starts accusing the patron of stealing. The store clerk yells racial slurs at the patron and threatens to call the police. The patron responds, "What is going on? What are you talking about? I didn't do anything! I purchased this!" The store clerk starts to argue back as he lifts the phone to call the police, and the patron replies, "Come on, I didn't do anything, ask the folks in the store."

What concerns you about intervening?

If you witnessed this, what would you do?

____ **A.** Walk up to the store clerk who accused him of stealing and say, "I saw him purchase the drink. You're wrongfully accusing this man, let him go on his way."

____ **B.** Pull out your phone and start recording the incident, and then share it with the patron to use as they see fit.

____ **C.** Wait until the situation has calmed down and then walk up to the patron and tell him you saw what happened and that it wasn't okay. Offer to be a witness for him if he wants one.

____ **D.** Walk up to the patron and ask him if he can help you find the nearest grocery store (that isn't that one).

____ **E.** Call the store, ask to speak to a manager or owner, and let them know what happened and that their clerk should be fired.

2 Your friend from high school, James, comments "haha so true" on a racist, anti-Asian meme trending on Facebook during the COVID-19 pandemic.

Your mutual friend from high school, Angie, who is Asian, explains how the meme is harmful. James responds by saying, "It's just a joke, don't be so sensitive."

What concerns you about intervening?

If you witnessed this, what would you do?

____ **A.** DM James: "Hey, I saw your comment to Angie. It surprised me, can we check in?" Then, reinforce Angie's point by explaining the impact that a comment like that can have.

____ **B.** Take a screenshot and keep a record of the incident in the event that it's needed.

____ **C.** DM Angie telling her you saw what happened and that it isn't okay. Ask how you can support her.

____ **D.** Post lots of GIFs or unrelated questions in the comments section to bury the negative comments.

____ **E.** DM another mutual friend from high school who is closer with James and ask him to explain to James why his comment was not okay.

3 Mark is new to the company and uses a wheelchair. He sometimes needs help reaching the coffee maker. When you walked into the break room this morning, you saw two other coworkers helping Mark use the coffee maker but making fun of him for not being able to reach it. Mark laughed but looked uncomfortable.

What concerns you about intervening?

If you witnessed this, what would you do?

___ **A.** Upon hearing these remarks, tell Mark's coworkers that they aren't being the kind and supportive colleagues that you know them to be.

___ **B.** After hearing this, write down the incident to provide Mark with a record of it if needed.

___ **C.** Check in with Mark afterward and say, "Hey, I heard that. It wasn't cool. Are you okay?"

___ **D.** Walk up to Mark, ask him about his day, and start a conversation about the most recent officewide memo.

___ **E.** Ask someone else in the break room to spill a drink or snack and provide a distraction.

4 You are at a bar having a quiet drink with some friends. A woman is sitting alone at the bar and another customer starts to give her a hard time. He reaches over, touches her, and occasionally talks about her body. The woman looks uncomfortable and moves further away, but the other customer continues with his comments.

What concerns you about intervening?

If you witnessed this, what would you do?

_____ **A.** Tell him, "I think it's time to find a new seat," and direct him toward an empty chair.

_____ **B.** Record the situation while you ask a friend to get help from the bartender.

_____ **C.** When she gets up to leave, walk with her toward the door and ask if she is okay.

_____ **D.** Physically stand between them and order a drink.

_____ **E.** Ask another patron if they feel comfortable helping the woman, or find a waiter or bartender and let them know what's happening.

5 You're at a pro-LGBTQ+ rally in a large park, where a group of anti-LGBTQ+ people are standing near your group, chanting disrespectful words.

Bobbi, an acquaintance and group member standing next to you, has chosen to participate by quietly holding a sign. One of the anti-LGBTQ+ people elevates their voice and focuses their gaze directly at Bobbi.

What concerns you about intervening?

If you witnessed this, what would you do?

___ **A.** Turn to Bobbi and say, "It looks like that person could use a break. But since they aren't taking one, maybe we should. I need to refill my water bottle; do you want to go with me?"

___ **B.** Take a video of the situation and give it to Bobbi as evidence of what happened.

___ **C.** Check in with Bobbi after the rally, tell them you noticed the focused attention, and see if they're okay or if they want to talk about it.

___ **D.** Ask Bobbi if they want to take a quick water or bathroom break with you.

___ **E.** Ask a member of your group to invite Bobbi to stand with other group members on the opposite side of the crowd.

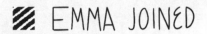

6 You're invited to a Slack channel about planning a team meetup. Upon joining, you see that two male colleagues you supervise have been messaging about a woman who joined the team last week, joking about how "hot" they find her and how they can't wait to be in the same city as she is. You notice that the woman has become silent in the group and stopped messaging back.

What concerns you about intervening?

If you witnessed this, what would you do?

___

_____ **A.** Respond, "Commenting on our coworkers' looks is inappropriate. Please stop it."

_____ **B.** Take a screenshot and keep a record of the incident in case it's needed.

_____ **C.** Check in with your new female colleague through a direct message in Slack to make sure they're okay and ask if there's any way you can support them.

_____ **D.** Change the subject entirely—start talking about places to meet up and give recommendations.

_____ **E.** Ask another person in the channel to directly intervene and let the two men know it's inappropriate to talk about people that way.

7 At a work training, a staff person who is transgender and uses they/them pronouns approaches a board member to ask what bathroom they should use, as they don't feel safe using a single-sex bathroom. The board member rolls her eyes and says, "I promise you, the ladies' room is perfectly safe. I was just in there and can attest there are no monsters lurking about."

What concerns you about intervening?

If you witnessed this, what would you do?

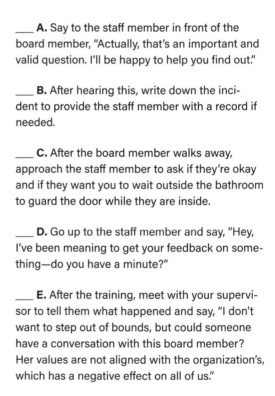

___ **A.** Say to the staff member in front of the board member, "Actually, that's an important and valid question. I'll be happy to help you find out."

___ **B.** After hearing this, write down the incident to provide the staff member with a record if needed.

___ **C.** After the board member walks away, approach the staff member to ask if they're okay and if they want you to wait outside the bathroom to guard the door while they are inside.

___ **D.** Go up to the staff member and say, "Hey, I've been meaning to get your feedback on something—do you have a minute?"

___ **E.** After the training, meet with your supervisor to tell them what happened and say, "I don't want to step out of bounds, but could someone have a conversation with this board member? Her values are not aligned with the organization's, which has a negative effect on all of us."

8 You go to a local park with your family to practice hitting tennis balls, and there are three teenage boys on bikes and scooters hanging around the wall you want to use. There is also an Asian family at the courts, and the boys are jeering at them, "You got corona? You got corona?" Soon, they start yelling, "You got corona! You mother——! You got corona! F— you! F— you!"

Then they speed by the family on their bikes and scooters. Another Asian family enters the park at that time and has the same thing happen to them.

What concerns you about intervening?

If you witnessed this, what would you do?

___ **A.** Yell to the teenagers on bikes, "Hey, hey! Leave those nice people alone!"

___ **B.** Share your story at StandAgainstHatred.org or RightToBe.org to build awareness.

___ **C.** Go up to both families and say, "I saw what happened and I'm so sorry. You don't deserve it."

___ **D.** Ask the family if they want to play tennis with you.

___ **E.** Ask another person or group in the park to intervene directly and tell the teenagers to leave other community members alone.

9 You're scrolling through Instagram and your friend Sam posted some cute pictures. As you press the "like" button and get ready to comment, you notice a few hateful comments like, "What are you, a boy or a girl?" as well as transphobic slurs.

What concerns you about intervening?

If you witnessed this, what would you do?

___ **A.** Comment to Sam, "Don't listen to what these folks are saying. I think your pictures are great!" Then tell the others that their behavior is transphobic.

___ **B.** Screenshot the comments, then report them.

___ **C.** DM Sam to check in and lift their spirits, then send them some uplifting content or resources on navigating online harassment.

___ **D.** Post a bunch of emojis and memes in the comments section so you drown out all the hate.

___ **E.** Report the abusive accounts to Instagram.

VVV23 ...

JEWS ARE
#@*/#!

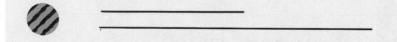

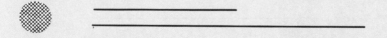
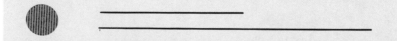

10 Your friend Victoria, who happens to be Jewish, posts a panicked tweet stating that several people have created impersonation accounts on Twitter using her name and photo. She says the impersonation accounts are tweeting homophobic slurs and anti-Semitic images, and she doesn't know what to do.

What concerns you about intervening?

If you witnessed this, what would you do?

___

___ **A.** Tweet "If you're as big a fan of Victoria V as I am, be sure to follow her REAL handle: @victoriav23. Abusive trolls are impersonating her—help me report this impersonation account @vvv23."

___ **B.** Go through her mentions, screenshot any abuse, and offer to give the record to her so she can decide if she wants to report it.

___ **C.** Offer to come over and help her strengthen her cybersecurity using a guide you found online. Bring ice cream.

___ **D.** Tweet "Hey, if you knew the real Victoria, you would know this is more her style." Post images of Victoria celebrating the Jewish holidays, or going to synagogue, or any other Jewish-positive content along with some LGBTQ+ affirming tweets or pictures.

___ **E.** Go through her mentions to find all the abusive accounts and rally some friends to join you in reporting them to Twitter.

How many times did you select each letter?

A _____ **B** _____ **C** _____ **D** _____ **E** _____

Once you've tallied your counts, turn to the Resources on page 196 to find out which of the 5Ds is your Superpower.

Top Superpower: _____

Backup Superpower: _____

While many of us have a Superpower we feel most comfortable using, it's important to understand that it may not always be the best intervention strategy for all instances of harassment we witness. In the next few chapters, we'll dig into the 5Ds of bystander intervention. While you're welcome to skip straight to the chapter that speaks specifically to your Superpower, we encourage you to check out all of the 5Ds.

DISTRACT

Distract relies on de-escalating harassment by drawing attention away from it. You can do this by creating a literal distraction, like dropping something, or by starting a conversation with the person being harassed.

Distract also serves as a way of showing the person who is causing harm that there is now another person there, which oftentimes will stop them in their tracks. The most important piece of advice is to remember that you are there to take care of the person experiencing harm. Don't engage with the person causing the harm.

DISTRACT IN PUBLIC

In public, you rarely know the people that you witness experiencing harassment. That can make it a lot trickier to assess the situation.

You may ask yourself:

- What's the backstory here? Who is harming whom?
- Is this going to escalate into violence?
- Why isn't anyone else doing anything?

Distract can be a great way to intervene in situations where the harassment is ongoing, but where you don't feel safe directly intervening.

Start a conversation with the person being harassed.

A common form of Distract is to start a conversation with the person being harassed about something completely unrelated. The goal is to build a safe space while denying the person doing the harassing of the attention they so desperately seek.

The beauty of a tactic like Distract is that you don't need to know who is in the right or wrong to create a distraction. You just need to be able to sense that something is off.

Here's a little inspiration from Twitter. Nicoletta (@nictoobomb) writes,

> *"Ricky was just acting like he wasn't my bf at the gym, saying to me 'you look nice in those leggings, can I take you out some time?'*
>
> *This girl (that I don't know) comes up to me and says, 'hey you ready to leave?' I informed her that he was my bf*
>
> *BUT GIRL I APPRECIATE YOU"*[43]

We love two things about this. First, the woman doesn't go up to Ricky and tell him off or lecture him about the impact of harassment. While that approach might be tempting, most people who harass aren't in their best "learning mindset" while harassing others. What she does is far more discreet, prioritizing above all else Nicoletta's, and her own, safety. She simply asks, "Hey, you ready to leave?"

The second thing we love is that she gets it wrong! It's a fear all of us have. But it actually doesn't matter that she gets it wrong. Like most of us, Nicoletta has probably been harassed hundreds of times in her life. So the experience of having someone support her, even when this one time it wasn't necessary, was still meaningful to her.

At one workshop a participant shared that they witnessed a woman being sexually harassed by a man near Columbia University. In an effort to de-escalate the situation, they walked up to the woman being harassed and said,

> *"Hey, oh my god, it's been such a long time since I've seen you! How is your family? What are you doing here? Did you finish your program? Come on, let's walk and talk. I have so much to share."*[44]

In this instance, they did not know each other, but the bystander's actions gave the woman a way out of the situation. The bystander actively built safe space and sought to get her out of the situation quickly and safely.

We've heard elders share that despite their concerns about safety stemming from the diminishing physical agility that often comes with age, they feel quite comfortable using approaches like Distract and find them effective.

Your identity shapes what forms of bystander intervention work best.

What works for one person may not work for another, and identity matters. For example, if you're intervening in a situation of sexist harassment by starting a conversation and you're a cis man, don't be surprised if the person being harassed assumes you're going to harass them, too. This may feel discouraging, but it shouldn't—the key is to build understanding and empathy for why the person being harassed holds that concern.

Sexual harassment can happen at the hands of men, women, and gender-expansive folks, but according to a 2018 study by Stop Street Harassment, 81 percent of women experienced some form of sexual harassment and/or assault compared with 43 percent of men. To successfully meet the needs of someone being harassed, you have to come to terms with a fundamental fact: Regardless of an individual's personal beliefs or behaviors, cis men, white folks, and others with societal privilege have historically had power over marginalized groups. Privileged groups have systematically used that power in ways that have ranged from dismissive to deeply violent.[45]

Identity and privilege aren't a simple one-to-one calculus, though. Identity is layered—it's possible to have privilege in one area, such as gender, but to be marginalized in another, such as race. In our day-to-day interactions, different aspects of your identity might influence whether someone views you as a threat.

As this seventy-three-year-old woman shared on Right To Be's website,

"When I see a young person in a situation of harassment, I go near her and say: 'Hey my niece, nice to see you.' The young person understands immediately.

We walk together [for] 5 minutes and the stupid person goes away.

This happens often. The young person is very surprised to be saved by a grandma."

Research by L'Oreal Paris and Ipsos shows that 79 percent of folks who experienced harassment say the situation improved when someone intervened, but only 25 percent say that someone has ever intervened on their behalf. Our job as bystanders (heck, as humans!) is to close that gap.[46]

Create a physical distraction.

Have you ever walked into an uncomfortable situation? One where you enter and whatever was happening before abruptly stops? Suddenly what you're doing or saying becomes the focus. Maybe the other person either walks away or loses their train of thought and their previous focus becomes an afterthought? Well, that's Distract in a nutshell. Sometimes just standing absentmindedly in the middle of things can be enough.

Let's say you're at a bar and you see someone being harassed at the counter. We've heard stories from folks who have simply gone up to the bar and wedged themselves between the person being harassed and the person doing the harassment, while simply saying "excuse me" and then signaling to the bartender they were ready to order. It's a simple enough action, but it can distract the person doing the harassing long enough to de-escalate the situation.

Let's look at another scenario. In a 2021 TikTok video that racked up more than 33 million views, a man named Brandon Robert was walking through a mall when he noticed a young woman being harassed.[47] He pulled out his phone and started videotaping himself.

"Oh my god, hi," Robert says in the video, talking to the woman. "How are you?"

She catches on immediately and acts like she knows him.

"My aunt is here, do you want to—," Robert asks, trying to give her an out to leave.

"Aunt Claire?" she replies. "Let's go."

As they are leaving, she says, "Oh my god, thank you so much."

Using the Distract method, Robert got this young woman to safety within a matter of minutes.

Make a scene.

We also recommend dropping things. Yes, dropping things.

Here's an example. Right To Be is partnered with L'Oréal Paris to train 1 million people globally to respond to street harassment when they see it or witness it. In the training, we show a video where an older woman drops a book right in between the woman experiencing harassment and the man doing the harassing. This provides an out for the woman being harassed. The older woman then turns and shares a knowing glance with the one experiencing harassment.

Beyond books, you can drop:

- **Your cell phone.** People will look to see if you broke it! (Make sure you have a good case for this one; once Emily broke her brand-new phone this way—but at least it stopped the harassment!)

- **Coins.** Most people will scramble to pick them up and hand them back to you. Of course, if you're living in a country where you use coins in higher denominations, you may want to keep a special pouch of lower denomination "harassment prevention coins" in your purse or wallet.

- **Your drink.** No one wants to get water or coffee on them, and most people will help you clean up a spill. Or at least try. If you've ever tried to go anywhere with a puking infant, you know firsthand how many people carry napkins in their purses.

And for all you theater lovers: Don't worry, we've got you. In a training at the Julliard School, one participant raised their hand and said "Miss! I know what I would do if I saw harassment happening!" They then offered, "I would break out in song and dance, and everyone would pay attention to me, instead of the harassment." For those of you who have the entire *Hamilton* musical memorized, this may be your big moment!

What not to do.

Here's where people get Distract wrong: They want to start a conversation about something random with the person doing the harassing (instead of the person being harassed). While this may disrupt the harassment, it also can be very confusing for the person being harassed. It can make them wonder, "Why does that racist/sexist/homophobe now have a new best friend, and still, no one is taking care of me?" It's best to start a conversation with the person being harassed and focus your energy on them.

The exception to that rule is if a conversation with the person harassing allows the person being harassed to get away. For example, if a store employee is following a Black shopper (this is a form of harassment—many store employees assume Black folks or other folks of color are going steal something), you may want to ask the store employee a series of questions about a particular product so that the other shopper can move through the store in peace.[48]

Starting a conversation with the person harassing is less likely to work in a scenario where the one being harassed can't escape easily or without consequence, such as on public transit or while waiting in line. In these situations, the person being harassed is forced to endure your pleasant line of questions to the person who just harassed them, while no one makes an effort to take care of them. Remember: Where you put your attention matters. If it's not prioritizing the person being harassed, it's not effective bystander intervention.

DISTRACT AT WORK

Intervening in workplace harassment requires navigating power and relationships. While your physical safety is (hopefully) less at risk at work than on the street, your job security and reputation are important considerations.

Meeting facilitation tactics are built for this.

Chances are, if you've ever facilitated a meeting, you've already used the Distract method at work. For example, let's say you're at a meeting and the conversation starts to veer toward disrespect. What you want to do with bystander intervention is the same thing you would want to do as a good facilitator: shift the energy.

Here are some strategies:

- **Ask a clarifying question.** "Bob, can you tell me more about the conclusions you drew from your research? What should we do next?"

- **Take a break.** "Okay! Let's take a quick break and meet back here in five."

- **Hear from everyone.** "I want to take the pulse of the whole room and hear from some of you who haven't spoken up yet. Let's go around in a circle and give one minute of feedback on this idea."

Even if you're not facilitating the meeting, requesting a quick break or asking clarifying questions are all within the realm of appropriate workplace etiquette.

One time at Right To Be, we brought in a couple of people who trained folks in bystander intervention—and almost instantly things went sideways.

Emily picked up on racial microaggressions so subtle that she started second-guessing herself, wondering if she was just misinterpreting what was said. She kept trying to make eye contact with the other team members to see if they noticed, too, but everyone had their head down—so she requested a quick bathroom break (Distract).

In the bathroom, the team agreed—there were multiple racial microaggressions at play and everyone was uncomfortable. We needed to stop the training. We came up with a plan, and Emily agreed to pull the trainer aside for a conversation (the Direct approach, which we'll learn about later).

If you don't feel comfortable asking for a break, you could also try spilling your drink on the table (watch out for the electronics, though!) or knocking over a cup full of pens on a conference table. This is especially effective in intense moments, like when someone is berating another employee in front of a team, or the harassment is ongoing. Once you create a "break" in the moment, then you can start looking toward the longer-term work of improving company culture and addressing disrespectful behavior.

How to Distract at work functions.

Distract can be effective at work functions where there are a lot of people watching and the stakes are high. You can't let harassment continue, but you may also be worried about "making a scene."

In one of our recent workshops, a woman shared a story from her recent company happy hour, where she saw a man harassing one of the women she worked with. The woman being harassed was clearly uncomfortable, but no one was intervening. It was time for the raffle to begin, so she used the opportunity to stop the harassment by asking the woman being harassed to pull the winning raffle ticket from the jar. All of a sudden, the attention of the room turned to her and the man harassing her quickly fled the scene. By shifting the energy of the room, she de-escalated the situation and got the harassment to stop.

Start a conversation.

Outside of the meeting context, you can take the same principle of "starting a conversation" that we discussed using in public space and apply it here, too. When you see harassment, try:

- "Hey, Maria, I need help on this report. Can you come over here and take a look at it?"

- "Bob, a customer in aisle three has a question, can you check on them?"

- "Tyrone, table three requested you. It seems urgent."

The same rules apply here as they do with Distract in Public: Don't start a conversation about something benign with the person doing the harassment as a way to de-escalate the situation if the person being harassed is stuck in the room with you both and unable to escape. Prioritize the person being harassed first and foremost.

DISTRACT ONLINE
Intervening in online harassment can be tricky, since the risks aren't always as visible. There are a number of well-publicized stories where someone intervened directly, and then the "angry online mob" started to attack the bystander with the same vigor with which they had attacked the person they were originally harassing. The internet allows for a level of coordination among strangers that can grow quickly and with little warning.

Because of this, most people will opt for a less obvious form of intervention online, like Distract. The idea of Distract is the same here, but the methods are different online. The good news is, the internet is a very distracting place! We've got a lot to work with.

Amplify the original post.

Here's the trick: You never want to amplify the abuse (don't give them the pleasure!). But by amplifying the original voice, you're saying, "Hey, we're going to let this person have their voice. We're going to like it, we're going to upvote it, we're going to retweet it, we're going to share it." Online harassment is like all forms of harassment: It is intended to silence people.

By lifting someone's voice, you're not only reminding the person being harassed that their voice matters, you're also showing the people who harass others that their attempts to silence another have backfired.

In 2016, we launched an online platform where people can share their experiences of online harassment and get support from a vetted community of bystanders. When it launched, we saw people eager to shut it down by organizing on forums like 4chan, Reddit, and Kiwi Farms. They tried everything, from mailing us hateful letters, to distributed denial-of-service (DDoS) attacks, to sending rape and death threats to our staff. They particularly took aim at the launch video we released, and the woman in it: a young queer woman of color named Marina Skylar. Within days of its launch, the video had 15,000 dislikes on YouTube and only several hundred likes—and hundreds of racist, sexist, and homophobic comments. We reached out to our community (a form of Delegate) and asked them to intervene using the Distract approach to upvote the video and share kind comments. They came in droves, as a "counterattack" to the hate.

You may wonder—what difference does it make? The hate still happened. But what we felt that day was similar to what we've heard echoed by thousands of others: a deep sense of care. Sure, people were still out there spewing hate at us. But there were also people poised and ready to show up for us. That care created resilience in our team. And yes, some of the main drivers of traffic to the platform continue to be forums like "Feminist and SJW Fails" (SJW stands for "social justice warrior" and is intended as a derogatory term deployed by people who are apparently not such big fans of social justice), but despite years of trolling, the platform is still going strong.

Draw attention away from the abuse.
It's really hard to be hateful while staring at a flood of photos of cute baby animals, GIFs of jumping goats, or elephants running through the wilderness in pink Converse high-tops. This type of content is not only de-escalating, it's funny. And the internet is fantastic at generating tons of it. As a bystander, you can use this type of content to intervene by flooding threads of hatred and abuse with threads of . . . singing puppies.

Humor has another role, too. The term "troll" is applied to people who harass online, but it was originally used as a way to self-describe by those people because they thought they were just being funny and "telling jokes." In online forums, you'll see streams of content about the so-called "snowflakes" who "can't take a joke," intended as defense of racist, sexist, and homophobic behavior. By using humor to create a distraction, you're turning trolling on its head.

Humor isn't the only way to create a distraction, however—sometimes it's just about banding together to spew truth. Jorge's cousin Diamond is a beauty blogger who creates live content, including makeup tutorials.[49] One day, two other beauty bloggers showed up to her session and immediately began trying to shame her and discredit her expertise. The audience saw what was happening and intervened. Instead of directly engaging with the people harassing her, without acknowledging the insulting comments, they began to chime in with ways that Diamond had helped them by commenting things like, "If you're looking for support on how to properly remove your make up check out the video from Friday," while others just started talking about how much they loved specific products that she had recommended to them. They commented things like, "Check Out Ulta's sale on the palette Diamond used in her video on Tuesday . . ." The other beauty bloggers eventually left. In this example, love and care—quite literally—chased away disrespect.

LAST WORDS ON DISTRACT

Distract invites a lot of creativity. When we poll our training attendees, this form of intervention is the top ranked Superpower: It disrupts ongoing harassment with little risk to the person intervening. Remember though, Distracting may not always be the right form of intervention for the moment. If the harassment is already over, it won't work. If you don't feel safe, Distract also may not fit. If Distract is your Superpower, we encourage you to check out the other Ds and commit to learning about your backup Superpower.

DELEGATE

Delegate is for the community organizer in each of us. At its core, it's about more than just finding someone else to help. It's about bringing people together under a united cause. It's about reminding the person being harassed that they aren't alone—but it's also about reminding you, the bystander, that you aren't alone, either.

Our favorite person to reach out to is the person right next to us. Like you, they are human—and as a human, they likely want to help other humans. Pulling them in with a quick, "Hey, do you see what's going on over there? Do you think that person's okay?" or, "I'm going to go and say something, will you come with me as backup?" helps build safety—and helps build community.

Sometimes when people think about Delegate, they think about calling the police if it's in public, or HR if it's at work—or reporting it on social media platforms online. While these are all viable options, they can fall short—especially for marginalized communities for whom these systems are not built.

At their worst, these systems can create further harm, such as in the case of a poorly handled HR investigation—or can cause irreparable damage, such as in the case of police violence and brutality. But it's worth noting that even a well-handled HR investigation or police interaction can be stressful and scary.

As with all the 5Ds, Delegate is about prioritizing the person being harassed. Given that people's identities, needs, wants, and preferences aren't always visible or clear, it's best to default to solutions that work for *most* people rather than solutions that only work for *some* people. When it comes to Delegate, this means checking in with the person being harassed before reaching out to systems of authority that have the potential to create further harm. The only exception to this rule is if it's a medical emergency and the person is unable to respond or otherwise indicate their needs. In these situations, calling for medical help is worth it.

DELEGATE IN PUBLIC

Delegate is a great option in situations where there are significant safety concerns. The safety concerns may be related to the situation (i.e., it's violent or police are involved), but it's also great in situations where you witness harassment directed at someone with whom you share identities. For example, if the harassment is ableist and you're also disabled, you may be nervous that the harassment will turn on you.

Before you get started in Delegation, own your expertise. So far you've not only identified the harassment for what it is, you've also understood intuitively the impact of harassment and the need for action. You've also identified your limits and listened to your instincts that you're not the right person to intervene. You're off to a great start.

Delegate to people you know.

Of course, the easiest people to delegate to are the people you already know. In one story we received at Right To Be, a woman was at a concert when she noticed another nearby woman looking uncomfortable as a man attempted to talk to her. She noted that something felt off. She kept watching, and when it escalated, she decided to act. She wrote:

"Then, the man opens his shirt and tries to pull the woman into him, against his very sweaty skin. The woman cowers, unsure what to do. I tell my husband what I see happening and that he needs to come with me now in case something happens."

Here we see her instinctively delegate a task to her husband. Although she doesn't explicitly state it, she likely did a quick safety assessment and realized that because this man was sexually harassing a woman, the harassment could turn toward her. Having a backup was a great idea. But take note of her Superpower in action here: It was she who noticed something was off, not her husband. We see, time and time again, that the people most likely to intervene are those who share an identity with the person being harassed—because they are the people who best know what to look for and often have firsthand experience with the impact of harassment. She continues:

> *"I walk over to the man and woman. I asked the woman first, 'Do you know him?' She responds that she does not know him. The woman moved away from him, now standing by my husband. I then look the man in the face and say, 'Excuse me, do you know her?' He said, 'No.' I respond with, 'Then you need to back off.' The three of us turned and immediately walked away. After creating some distance, the woman turns to me and says, 'Thank you so much!'"*

Once this bystander confirmed the support of her husband, her personal safety assessment shifted and she felt comfortable jumping in directly to intervene, set a boundary with the person doing the harassment, and take care of the person being harassed by getting them out of the situation.

Here's another example where two friends banded together to intervene on behalf of their other friends, but this time, the harassment turned on them:

> *A few years ago, a Filipino friend and I (Japanese-American) were riding the NYC subway with some female work friends. The train was semi-crowded, so he and I were standing apart from our friends, who were seated.*
>
> *A man who was closer to our friends began to verbally sexually harass them. My friend and I looked at each other and silently decided to move closer to our friends and stand in front of them. We began a loud conversation with them—the idea being to drown out the man's harassment. I don't remember what exactly we talked about, but at one point we did talk loudly about how sexist men are likely*

insecure—admittedly, this wasn't the smartest thing to do as it just escalated the man's anger.

He redirected his verbal invective toward my Filipino friend and I—so, the comments became more racist than sexist. My friend and I both train in martial arts and were probably feeling overconfident, but we focused on the conversation with our friends while keeping an eye on the man out of the corner of our eyes. The man eventually lost interest and got off the train."

Here we see Delegate used alongside Distract. Delegation doesn't always mean finding someone else to intervene instead of you; it can also mean finding someone else to intervene *with* you. Here, the two friends banded together to create a distraction by starting a conversation with the people being harassed.

Delegate to a stranger.

Delegating to a stranger can be incredibly effective, but it is important to remember that they may not be familiar with bystander intervention. They also may not have much practice showing up in support of people who aren't like them. Here are a few things to look for when you're finding a stranger to delegate to:

- **They are paying attention.** In a crowded environment, the right person to delegate to is probably the person most closely watching what's going on (as opposed to the person buried in their phone, book, or with headphones on). If they're paying attention, that means they have context, and at least to a certain extent, they care.

- **They understand why it's not okay.** Sometimes people may not perceive a situation as harassment, even if it clearly is. For example, able-bodied people can watch other able-bodied people address disabled adults who use wheelchairs as if they were children, using a "baby" voice, and perceive that as "just being nice"—whereas another disabled person can more clearly identify

When the Harassment Turns on You

If you intervene and the harassment turns on you, here are some tips:

- **Trust your instincts.** Listen to your gut. There is no "right" or "perfect" response to harassment; however, studies show that having some kind of response (either in the moment or later) can reduce the trauma associated with harassment. If you decide to respond, do it for you.

- **Decide if you want to respond and how.** It's completely valid not to respond. If you do, consider telling the person harassing you exactly what you want them to do and why: "I need you to get away from me and my friends. We're not interested in speaking with you." You might also try engaging bystanders by telling them what's going on and what they can do to help—for instance, asking, "Can you make sure this man doesn't come near my friends and me?" You might also decide to document the situation. Even if you never do anything with it, having evidence of what you experienced is a powerful feeling (more on this later).

- **Practice resilience.** There is strength in recognizing that harassment hurts. Don't shove it down and pretend it didn't happen. Instead, take care of yourself. Tell your friends what happened, map your story on RightToBe.org if it helps, breathe deep, and remember that you are strong. If possible, you may also want to consider finding a licensed mental health professional.

that behavior as ableist. If someone questions if what's unfolding is "really harassment" or not, try someone else.

- **They are eager to help.** A quick "check-in" can help you decide if someone will be a good delegate. Ask them something like, "Do you see what's going on over there? Do you think they are okay? Would you be willing to help?" As with anything else, make sure the person fully (and enthusiastically!) consents to intervening.

Once you've found the right person, the next step is to communicate exactly what you want them to do. You'll see that Delegate often works hand-in-hand with another of the 5Ds. For example, you might:

- **Combine Distract with Document:** "I'm going to create a distraction by dropping my water bottle to try and de-escalate the situation. Can you hang here and have my back in case things escalate?"

- **Combine Document with Delegate:** "I'm going to tell that man they need to leave that person alone. Can you document the situation so we can give them the footage afterward in case they want to report him?"

- **Combine Direct with Delegate:** "Would you mind telling that person to leave him alone? I don't feel comfortable saying anything, but I can hang here and document it discreetly just in case he decides to report it later."

If you're someone who is comfortable with Direct intervention, you may find yourself delegating after you've already intervened. You might ask one person to get some water for the person who was harassed. You might ask another person to stand next to the person doing the harassing and make sure they don't go near the person they were harassing again.

Leverage privilege when you Delegate.

Privilege is a set of unearned benefits that you have as a result of your identity. Allyship in action looks like using those benefits to support others who don't receive them. For example, people with *white privilege* might be great allies in disrupting race-based harassment, because by design race-based harassment is unlikely to turn on them, and the police are less likely to be called on them. Similarly, *male privilege* can be effectively leveraged

to address gender-based harassment: A sexist male will likely heed the guidance of another man better than he would that of any woman or gender-expansive person.

Don't be shy about tapping in some men, white folks, cis folks, or able-bodied people the next time you see harassment happening. It shouldn't be on folks who disproportionately experience harassment to do all the work.

The limits of authority.

Public transit can be a great place to delegate interventions to those around you, as there are often many, and it's hard not to watch what's going on in such a contained space. It is also oftentimes easy to find an authority figure on public transit, such as a train conductor, ticket agent, or transit police. Delegating to a person with authority in that space is not always a simple calculus, though.

Here's a story that took place on the New York City subway system, where a (presumably) Latina woman was harassed while a Black person tried to intervene:

"A woman on the subway was standing as a man tried to get her attention for over ten minutes while she ignored him. He was whistling and waving at her as if he were calling a dog. She moved away but he didn't stop, and I told him to cut it out. His response to me was, 'What are you gonna do, take a knee like a Black person?'"

Here, we see the harassment pivot from sexist to racist like the flip of a switch. What starts off as the harassment of a Latina woman based on sexism quickly pivots to the harassment of a Black person (the bystander). Then, she too starts being harassed based on race:

"He then went on a rant about how there are too many Hispanics and Blacks, and then taunted me to call the police

on him, saying, 'I'm a cop.' He tried again to get the woman's attention by speaking bad Spanish to her and saying, 'I know you're a Dominicana.' An MTA [Metropolitan Transit Authority] attendant happened to come to the car soon after, and I asked if anything could be done about that man. She said nothing could be done unless he touched someone."

Even the most well-intentioned transit employee has limits. They are forced to subscribe to the rules of the system whether or not those rules are fair or right. Failure to comply with the rules of the system may pose a risk to their job security.

In our work with public transit employees, we learned how they too are subject to extreme forms of harassment on the job, with little recourse or support from their employer. For instance, as drivers, they are told never to leave the driver's seat of the bus while on duty under any circumstances. One bus driver told us a story in which an irate rider urinated on her while she was in the driver's seat of the bus. In this extreme situation, she decided to get up to go to the nearest restroom and clean herself off. She was later reprimanded for leaving the bus unattended and received little or no sympathy for the harassment that she had to endure.

When working within flawed systems that aren't built to prevent harassment on multiple sides, even solution-oriented decision-making is often limited and imperfect. In another story, a person decided to photograph someone harassing others and show the photo to the train conductor to get help. They wrote:

"I made the conductor face us, not the guy in the car, and showed him the photo of the guy. The conductor took a photo of my photo on the phone. He said something into his walkie-talkie. Then he said he had a plan. He suggested that all of us get out at the next stop . . . and do it right before the

train closes the doors, so the guy can't jump up and follow us. On his cue, we left the train and watched the guy and the train leave from the platform."[50]

They expressed gratitude and caught the next train. It was a good result, but it begs a deeper question: Why is it more normalized to expect the people who experience harassment to catch the next train—and not the people who harass others?

At Right To Be, we don't endorse increasing the criminalization of harassment, but we do endorse prioritizing the needs of people who experience harassment over the impulses of those who harass. When we tell people who are experiencing harassment to change their behavior in order to "avoid" harassment, we put the blame in the wrong place. Ultimately, it's the responsibility of the person who harasses to stop.

If you're considering contacting the police in an instance of harassment, we strongly recommend giving agency to the person experiencing harassment by letting them make the decision about whether to report it. The police have a long history of harassment and brutality, especially toward communities of color. In fact, they don't even have a great track record of de-escalating conflict—in New York City, for example, the police force did not receive conflict de-escalation training until 2021.[51]

In our work with trans and gender-expansive communities of color, who represent some of the people most at risk of harassment, we have heard that even as the police are an absolute concern, delegating to people in other positions of authority, like store managers, transit workers, educators, doctors, etc., doesn't always feel safe, either. Those people can also be part of biased systems eager to criminalize others: For example, teachers with racial bias that are more likely to suspend Black and brown students than white students, transit workers and private bus companies that threaten the safety of undocumented commuters by harassing riders about their identification "papers," and medical professionals who misgender their trans patients.

In a medical emergency, you may need to call for an ambulance, and in most parts of the world that will signal the police to come, too. When someone is hurt to the point that they can't verbally or otherwise indicate what they need in terms of support, calling is worth it—but the rest of the time, keep in mind that the best person to delegate to is probably right beside you.

DELEGATE AT WORK

At work, employees are under a lot of pressure to delegate the handling of harassment to human resources departments or their managers. This can be an effective strategy, but it is nevertheless limited.

Dealing with Human Resources.

Harassment can have a chilling effect on a team. Even if it hasn't happened to you directly, knowing it happens to others at your workplace can leave you feeling vulnerable and unsafe. If you're considering reporting an incident of harassment to HR, know that most human resources departments will accept reports from bystanders, with the understanding that it's in their best interest to address harassment quickly. If you're a manager, you are bound by US law to report incidents and observations of harassment, even if you believe they are insignificant or just attempts at humor.

But for the rest of us, it's worth checking in with the person being harassed before reporting an incident to HR. Approaching HR with an incident report will likely kick off an investigation. Reaching out first affords them a heads up about the possibility of involving HR, and you can learn more about how they would like the situation to be handled. For example, they may request to stay anonymous. Or they may feel bolstered by your allyship and request that you both file the report together. It is key to give the person who was harassed the power to choose the next step.

If you do report an incident to HR, here are a few more best practices:

First, do not tell anyone else at work. It's not your story to share. Oftentimes, this kind of information can travel through the rumor mill in ways that aren't productive. For example, when Emily was sexually harassed at work, witnesses not only reported the incident to management; they also told the entire workplace about it. While their intentions may have been good, Emily's coworkers started to look for ways in which Emily had been "asking for it" as a way of reassuring themselves: "Well, just because this happened to her doesn't mean it will happen to me." It may have been a self-protective instinct, but their reaction was to shame and ostracize Emily. The response from her team was far more traumatizing than the original incident and the investigation into it.

Second, your role as an ally doesn't end when you report harassment to HR. Investigations can be hard, retraumatizing, and if done poorly, they can even create new trauma. Hang in there with the person who was harassed. Check in with them regularly and give them extra support and care however you can. If you're their manager, ask them if they need adjustments in their workflow or days off, if possible, to take care of themselves.

Delegating to your colleagues.

As we've said before, choosing the person next to you as a delegate to intervene can be an effective strategy. Perhaps the person next to you has a better relationship with the one who just uttered that microaggression in a meeting. Maybe their position or identity would allow them to more readily ask, "What did you mean by that?" This is also a good place to leverage your allies. If you witness a racist microaggression, consider nudging your white coworkers to say something. If it's an ableist form of harassment, get your able-bodied coworkers to step up and intervene. Unlike when you witness harassment in public spaces, at work you probably have a better sense of which of your team members are your best allies.

In one workplace we trained, we met a "super-intervener" who intervened in situations of harassment, disrespect, and microaggression so often she started worrying that upper management would tag her as a "trouble-maker." She started delegating others to intervene with different forms of Distract. For instance, if she saw someone being verbally berated near the kitchen, she would ask her coworkers to create a distraction: for example, "Hey Bob, can you tell Paige I need to see her?" The best part about this approach is that "Bob" had no idea he was de-escalating a situation—he was just doing what he had been asked to do.

If disrespect, harassment, or microaggressions happen in a meeting, consider delegating the meeting facilitator to intervene. You could text them, DM them online, or just ask them, "Can we have a five-minute break?" This is a discreet way of addressing harassment without confronting it head-on or being labeled a so-called "troublemaker."

DELEGATE ONLINE

Those who harass online go to great lengths to self-organize and coordinate their efforts, so why shouldn't those of us who experience online harassment do the same?

Engage your networks.

Consider reaching out to supportive communities, like Listservs, your close friends' group chat, your private Facebook community, etc., to sound the alarm. Support might look like amplifying the voice of the person being harassed, or reporting the harassment to the platform's moderators. Among many professions where online harassment is common (like journalism, content creation, and activism), it's not uncommon to see notes sent out across Listservs like "My friend is being impersonated online & she can't get the account removed. Can you join me in reporting it?"

Julia loffe, a journalist who covers national security and foreign policy, often receives anti-Semitic attacks on Twitter. In one example, she retweeted screenshots of the harassment with the comment "Good morning, from your neighborhood Trump trolls!" The screenshots included a photo of her speaking on camera, photoshopped with an image of the Star of David used in German concentration camps. Later, she shared a screenshot of Twitter's response that there was "no violation of policies," along with the comment, "I reported a user who said 'f— off Jew' to me and this was Twitter's response. Really?" Sometimes the downside of reporting your own experiences of online harassment is that you might receive an email from the social media platform that essentially says, "We don't think this is harassment"—which is invalidating and can be traumatizing in its own

right. But her community responded en masse. Followers like @AliceWG responded and wrote, "@juliaioffe Reported every one whose username I could see for targeted harassment. Keep fighting the good fight."[52] Twitter finally responded by closing some of the harassing accounts.

In another well-publicized example, Milo Yiannopoulos, the former editor of *Breitbart*, was removed from Twitter after publicly harassing actress Leslie Jones, the only Black woman in the all-women cast of the *Ghostbusters* remake.[53] Yiannopoulos quote-tweeted her tweets with comments like, "Barely literate. America needs better schools!" and images that said "Who you gonna call? Weightwatchers!" Jones's fanbase responded by reporting Yiannopoulos and flooding the hashtag #LoveforLeslieJ. Thousands of tweets rolled in, drowning out Yiannopoulos and his followers, and setting a positive and supportive tone on the internet.[54]

Don't forget the screenshot.

One last pro-tip on reporting harassment to social media platforms: It's great to pair this strategy with screenshotting, grabbing the hyperlink, and Documenting the harassment for the person being harassed. This can be helpful in the event that anything is deleted, so that evidence remains for a potential report in case it escalates.

LAST WORDS ON DELEGATE

Delegate is not about just passing the buck to the next person to take on harassment. It's about building a community of interveners. Sometimes that can mean enlisting systems and structures, like security guards, HR, or TikTok, but often it's just about getting the person next to you involved. The best way to internalize the impulse to intervene as a bystander is to see other people doing it. Delegate gives us the ability to model and teach bystander intervention to others. It's about clearly and publicly establishing a norm: Harassment isn't acceptable, and hate-based violence has got to stop.

DOCUMENT

In the twenty-first century, our cell phone cameras have captured so many human rights abuses. But bystander intervention's primary goal is to give power back to the person who was harassed.

Like the other methods of intervention we've introduced, Document works well in combination with other approaches. There are two major guidelines when it comes to documentation. First, make sure someone is already intervening in another way—it doesn't help someone being harassed if you stick a camera into their traumatic moment while no other support is offered to them. In fact, someone being harassed might be further traumatized if they are watching you film them being harmed while doing nothing else to help. If you don't feel safe intervening, consider delegating first. Once you've done that, you can start documenting.

Second, always give any documentation you create to the person being harassed. This is not your opportunity to post something new on your social media feed. Give *them* the option to share it on social media—or to take it to the bus company where it happened, or give it to the local media to create awareness, or whatever else they may want to do. Your role is to give them the option to choose. Give them their power back. The choice is theirs.

Document has helped spark movements, change narratives, and offer accountability for people who experience disrespect, harassment, or violence. While there are many nuances due to varying laws around recording or getting permission to record in different spaces, it remains an extremely powerful tool. Document allows you to transport others when sharing your experiences, in a way that no amount of words or storytelling can accomplish. It also provides folks with concrete proof of their experiences in ways previously impossible.

DOCUMENT IN PUBLIC SPACE

Document is near and dear to our hearts because it is integral to our organization's beginnings. In 2005, Thao Nguyen, a young Asian woman, bravely stood up to the person harassing her—an older, white, upper middle class raw-foods restaurant owner—who terrified her by masturbating while sitting across from her on the subway. She took his photo with her phone camera, and when the police ignored her report of the incident, she posted the photo on Flickr. From there, it eventually made it to the front page of the *New York Daily News*, where it incited a citywide conversation about street harassment. Seven young people (of which Emily was one) were particularly inspired by Nguyen's story. They decided to apply her model to all forms of street harassment and to document these experiences on a public blog.[55]

How to Document safely.

As with all forms of bystander intervention, prioritize your safety when using Document. Many worry that if someone sees them filming harassment, their phone might be grabbed, or someone may become violent. If this is your concern, hold it as true. Rest assured, that doesn't mean you can't Document.

Many people document harassment discreetly. In a world where it's normal to see people's faces buried in their phones, it's easy to fly under the radar while documenting. Try acting like you're checking your email or texting. Some people try pretending that they are taking a selfie. Many people choose to document from a seated position (such as on a train, or in a waiting room) because it's easier to film and hold your phone at an angle where no one can see your screen, and it looks like you're just playing with your phone.

How to capture effective footage.

Here are some other things to consider when documenting harassment that we learned from our partners at WITNESS:[56]

- **Hold your phone horizontally.** Holding the phone horizontally may be less discreet than holding the phone vertically, so assess how drawing attention

Learn Your Local Laws

Before getting started, find out your local laws around filming in public space. In the United States, laws vary from state to state, but generally it is legal to film in public spaces, as it is a part of your First Amendment rights—as long as a "public" place is truly public, like the street, the subway, or a park, because there is no "reasonable expectation of privacy." Private businesses, however, like restaurants, gyms, or stores, can set their own rules. If they ask you to stop filming and leave and you don't, you could be charged for trespassing.

In some cities and countries, such as Italy and the Netherlands, you can't film in public spaces without both parties' consent. You can record audio without both parties' consent, but if you make it public to anyone beyond you, the person speaking, and the court, it's considered "slander." In these situations, however, don't give up on documenting—resort to pen and paper. Write down the streets, the time, business names, license plates, and other details you can gather.

In the US, election locations are a gray area: Are they public or not? The laws vary greatly from state to state. In our work to stop voter harassment at the polls, we learned that in some states, there is no law against filming at a polling site, while in others you can't film in the room where you vote. And in some states, you can't film within a hundred feet of a polling site.[57] Taking the time to learn your local laws will help you feel more confident if and when you choose to use Document.

to yourself might impact your safety. If you're able, hold your phone steady and use slow and steady pans instead of quick movement. Sometimes in the middle of a situation of harassment, our adrenaline and nerves can kick in—try to avoid shaky footage or quick and sudden movements that make it more difficult to see what is happening.

- **Get the details.** If it feels safe, WITNESS recommends filming for longer than ten seconds so the viewer has enough footage to decipher the situation. You'll also want to capture things like the number of people present, license plate numbers of cars involved, street signs, landmarks, or exteriors of buildings to help determine location.

- **Turn on your phone's location services.** Many smartphones geolocate files to where they were created. You can always turn them off afterward to protect your digital security.

Whether or not you are able to record everything on video, you can still create a voice memo or use the timeless pen and paper method to write down everything you remember.

Use Document to address police-sponsored violence and brutality.

Too often, calling the police has been weaponized against historically marginalized communities. One of many examples is the case of Amy Cooper and Christian Cooper (no relation) in Central Park, New York, in 2020.

Christian (a Black man) was birdwatching, and he asked Amy (a white woman) to put her dog on a leash in compliance with park rules. Amy became angry, which made Christian nervous, so he started filming. Amy told Christian that she was going to call the police and "tell them there's an African-American man threatening my life." At this point, Christian was several feet, if not yards, away from her, and he had already told her, "Please don't come close to me," when she began approaching him. Still, Amy dialed 911 and told them that an African-American man was threatening her and her dog. Because Christian caught what happened on video, it was later viewed by millions online and across news media.[58]

In addition to white people's weaponization of the police against people of color, there is also a long history of the police themselves lying about people of color. Cameras can't single handedly solve this, of course, and they don't always give us the full story. But they are a more reliable narrator than most. Using Document to intervene in police violence not only illuminates injustice, it also has a proven track record of aiding in holding police accountable for their actions.

In the trial of Derek Chauvin, the officer who murdered George Floyd in 2020, video recordings from various bystanders were used to create a more detailed account of events. This led the jury to find Derek Chauvin guilty of second-degree unintentional murder, third-degree murder, and second-degree manslaughter.[59] The footage showed bystanders pleading with Chauvin to remove his knee from Floyd's neck. A seventeen-year-old Black teen named Darnella Frazier captured the pivotal documentation. Frazier later won an honorary Pulitzer Prize in journalism for her heroic action.

Firefighter Genevieve Hansen pleaded to intervene and help Floyd, but she was denied and threatened. Instead, she captured footage of the murder. "There was a man being killed. I would have been able to provide medical attention to the best of my abilities, and this human was denied that right."[60] Had Chauvin and the other officers listened, Hansen and others could have saved Floyd's life.

While the documentation did not save George Floyd's life, it started a national movement and conversation around police brutality and its effects on Black communities. Black communities have been crying out for an end to police violence and injustice since long before Floyd was killed. But with the documentation of Chauvin brutalizing and murdering Floyd, the entire nation was collectively confronted with the harsh realities of racism, police brutality, and violence toward communities of color. This led to protests and initiatives nationwide, which triggered pushes for police reform and conversations to reimagine public safety solutions that prioritize communities and do not involve hyper-policing. Community-based solutions such as bystander intervention training, as well as dispatching crisis units equipped with social workers and mental health professionals

ST ONE

ST TWO

to people experiencing mental health crises, have become viable policy alternatives to policing—not just "fringe" ideas.[61]

While this is just the beginning, documentation is a powerful tool for enacting tangible change by spreading awareness of injustices. Moments create movements, and in this instance, the video of Chauvin's actions toward Floyd propelled a movement into action. The reverberations continue to be felt globally.

Document empowers people to hold a lens up to their experience—and to their communities. In some cases, this has helped increase awareness of the pervasive harm. During the COVID-19 pandemic, the prevalent use of Document to capture injustice and violence against members of the AAPI (Asian American and Pacific Islander) community led people to take action by donating to AAPI organizations, getting trained in bystander intervention, and demanding government accountability. Especially in communities of color like the AAPI community, where instances of harm were occurring but weren't as commonly documented, we saw this form of intervention begin to not only raise awareness but also to empower people to share their experiences in an effort to demand change.

DOCUMENT AT WORK

Workplaces are considered a private space, which means you can't legally document harassment using your phone, camera, or video equipment without the consent of all parties involved. But that doesn't mean documentation isn't still a great strategy. It just requires a different approach: writing things down.

Write it all down.

When harassment happens in the workplace, there are many policies and procedures to navigate. For example, if you tell a manager or HR person in the United States that you experienced "harassment," "discrimination," or "retaliation"—or even if you don't use those specific words, but your employer believes your experiences constitute a form of harassment, discrimination, or retaliation—they are legally required to run an investigation.

Know Your Rights

When using Document to intervene in police brutality in the United States, there are a few special considerations to keep in mind (in other countries, research your local laws):

- Keeping a safe distance is especially important because if you are too close, police can arrest you for obstruction of justice. There is no standardized distance at which they gain the ability to do this, so to be safe, we recommend about twenty feet.

- You do not need to hide the fact that you are filming because it is protected by your First Amendment rights. As public servants, the police have no expectation of privacy while they are conducting their duties.

- Police typically cannot search your phone without a warrant or make demands that you delete information. Still, there have been instances of police misconduct where police officers have erased footage of an incident without the person's knowledge or consent. If the police try to confiscate your phone, gently but firmly remind them they need a warrant.

- Always keep a passcode on your phone instead of using advanced security features like fingerprints or facial recognition. Here's why: Under the Fifth Amendment, you have the right not to self-incriminate, which means you do not have to reveal any information that may incriminate you—including the passcode to your phone. If you have facial recognition or fingerprint security measures, the police may be able to circumvent your Fifth Amendment rights by forcibly using your face or your fingerprints to open your phone and remove the content.

- Do not alter the original file name or footage on your phone. If you do, it can be considered doctored footage and rendered inadmissible in court.

In most states and workplaces, your coworkers can also report your experience of harassment to HR or management without your prior knowledge or consent (though as discussed in the Delegate chapter, it's always best to check in first before reporting on someone else's behalf).

Harassment can be hard to prove from a legal standpoint, and laws vary regionally. But even if the harassment isn't determined to match the legal definitions (which—as we've mentioned—are limited), good employers will still seek to meaningfully address harassment. But they will be cautious of being sued for wrongful termination if they fire someone without sufficient evidence of harassment. So, having witnesses can bolster your case—and help you feel less intimidated and alone during a workplace investigation.

Having details of incidents of harassment, discrimination, and/or microaggressions is key to proving a "hostile work environment" if the person who was harassed decides to report the incidents. When you witness harassment in the workplace, take notes while it is happening or as soon as possible afterward to guarantee the best possible recollection of the story (in legal terms, these are called contemporaneous notes). You should write down:

- Where and when did it happen?

- What was said and/or done?

- Who else was there? Who else became aware afterward (if anyone)?

- How did it make you feel? Was there any effect on your work performance, relationships, confidence, creativity, etc., as a result?

- Is there any record of the harassment? This could include documentation of the actual harassment (e.g., an email), but it can also be confirmation of details of the harassment (e.g., a due date for an assignment that is relevant to your story).

- Are you aware of other incidents of harassment related to this one (i.e., did this person harass anyone else)?

Document as much detail as possible. While you may not be able to use your phone to record the incident, you might take photos of any inappropriate materials. Saving your notes, photos, screenshots, etc., to external storage can help ensure you have continued access to these materials in the event that they are confiscated for an investigation.

The trick to Documenting in the workplace is to write things down as quickly as possible. We often think we'll remember, but when it comes to traumatic situations, our brains sometimes like to do us a favor by blurring our memories. This blurring of memory is common with sexual assault survivors, war veterans, and others who have experienced extreme trauma, but it can also happen to bystanders who may experience an incident as secondary trauma. Secondary trauma, also known as "vicarious trauma," is how we're affected emotionally and psychologically when we're exposed to the suffering of others. It can show up as feelings of mental, physical, and/or emotional exhaustion when engaging empathetically with someone who has experienced trauma—and it's common. To mitigate the impacts, it's best to write down the details of harassment as quickly as possible.

Just because you don't film it doesn't mean it won't be filmed.

Customers at stores have historically broken laws that prohibit photography in private businesses (for the most part, without consequence) to document harassment happening to employees. At the height of COVID-19, we witnessed a number of videos where frontline and essential workers were harassed for asking members of the public to adhere to safety regulations. On April 30, 2020, an Austin park ranger was pushed into a lake after asking a group of visitors to stay six feet away from each other.[62] Later that summer, on June 22, a Florida man was caught on camera physically pushing an employee at a Walmart for asking him to wear a mask. Similarly, that same month a white woman berated and cursed at a 7-Eleven employee of color because he asked her to wear a mask.[63]

The rise in violent incidents at stores was widely reported on news media and pushed local officials, such as the mayor of San Antonio, Texas, to make statements on behalf of businesses, supporting their right to deny service over refusal to comply with mask requirements. "Let's be clear," Mayor Ron Nirenberg said, "the store has the authority to require a patron to wear a mask. . . . Protesting the requirement doesn't confer the right for someone to trespass. It doesn't confer the right to disrupt the business and doesn't confer them the right to assault someone."

At Right To Be, we saw a dramatic increase in demand for conflict de-escalation training for frontline workers. The outpouring of support for frontline workers was undoubtedly bolstered by the live video footage documented by customers and ultimately publicized across social and traditional media outlets.

DOCUMENT ONLINE
It's best practice to keep screenshots and hyperlinks of any online harassment—even if you don't think it will escalate and you don't want to report it to law enforcement. The trouble is that capturing such information can deepen trauma for those harassed by increasing their exposure to the hateful material.

Some journalists "play defense" by documenting harassment directed toward them in the event that it escalates. In a *Vanity Fair* article, journalist Hilary Sargent shared, "Finding a group of people that you can trust to collect that information, but that's not a group of people who are also dealing with it themselves, is really hard." According to the article, Sargent's experience with harassment drove her to step back significantly from freelance writing, a fate that possibly could have been prevented had bystanders stepped up to screenshot and grab hyperlinks of all the harassment she was facing, allowing her to prioritize her own healing.[64]

How to document harassment online.
Documenting harassment with both screenshots and hyperlinks is especially important because in the event that it is reported to moderators, they generally remove it, thus destroying the evidence. Before doing this, if you're able, ask the person if this support would be helpful. If you're unable to ask them (maybe they have gone offline, etc.), it's okay to go ahead and document their harassment—you'll just want to put the screenshots

and hyperlinks into a folder and email the entire folder to them with a message like, "I want to ensure you have evidence of this abuse. Attached are screenshots to file away." It helps to hide the evidence under a layer of protection instead of copy-pasting it directly into an email, so that the person being harassed is given some agency and can control when they see or engage with the evidence (if they choose to at all).

Bystander platforms can help.

Another option if you're being harassed online is to visit Right To Be's website, where you can enlist the support of a vetted community of bystanders to screenshot the harassment on your behalf and have it saved on the back-end of the system for when (and if) you want to review it.

Tactics like "blocking" (where you block users from being able to contact you at all) or "muting" (where users can still contact you; you just don't see what they have to say) are tempting, but they can mask the presence of deeper, more serious threats. If someone is committed to harming you, your family, or your reputation, the threat isn't necessarily going to go away. Offer to monitor mentions and document harassment—and, importantly, encourage the person being harassed to take a break from the internet to take care of themselves.

LAST WORDS ON DOCUMENT

Document is a complex tool, but nonetheless a powerful one. Because it requires navigating more laws, systems, and standard practices than other forms of intervention, many people shy away from Document. But you shouldn't: The truth has power. Stories have power. And it can be used very effectively in combination with other bystander intervention techniques. Document combines hard evidence with the narrative of lived experience not only to shake the foundations of racism, sexism, homophobia, and hate—but also to break them.

DELAY

Imagine this: someone hurls a slur at you—and everyone is watching. No one does anything or checks in on you. They all act like nothing happened. You start to imagine that because they aren't saying anything, they probably agree with this person. Your sense of safety and self-worth plummets.

Quite simply, Delay is about checking on the person who was harassed after it's over. It's a way of validating someone's experiences: Yes, that happened. No, it wasn't okay. And no, you're not alone. Research we conducted in collaboration with Cornell University showed that as little as a knowing glance can reduce trauma related to harassment. And that's something all of us can do, but too often we don't.

Instead, we tell ourselves, "Well, it's over. The slur has been hurled. The microaggression has been uttered. Nothing to be done now." Sometimes people even worry that bringing attention to the harassment can make things worse by bringing more shame. However, that concern doesn't necessarily match up with the lived experiences of most people who have been harassed—those of us who have experienced harassment already know we were harassed, regardless of how much attention others pay. What we don't know is if anyone cares.

Delay reminds people being harassed that they aren't alone. It sends them the message: You aren't alone, and you don't have to go through this alone. There are other people out there standing up against this kind of hate; there are people out there who see you and hear you; there are people out there who get it.

DELAY IN PUBLIC

Sometimes harassment happens so quickly that by the time you're actually able to intervene, it's over. Other times, you freeze as a witness, and it isn't until the harassment is over that you actually manage to act. In these situations, Delay is a great approach. It's such a simple form of bystander intervention that it's easy to forget or skip—but when it's used, its impact is felt immediately.

What to say to someone who has just been harassed.

Here's a simple way to get started with Delay—just ask "Are you okay?" Those three magic words can go a long way. Take it from a woman who shared her story with Right To Be: After insults were hurled at her, she wrote, "a couple of passersby witnessed what happened and very kindly asked me if I was okay (I cannot stress how important it is to get this kind of support from strangers)."[65]

It really is that simple, but that doesn't mean it doesn't take courage. Another person wrote that they witnessed a woman repeatedly decline a man's persistent advances. They wrote, he "finally walked away to the other end of the car. I smiled at her and said, 'I've got your back.' She was happy, and we chatted a bit about how annoying and creepy men can be. It really felt great that I was going to help her, and I felt strong and really good about myself."

I've got your back. Another simple four-word phrase that can mean the world to someone who's just been harassed.

Here's another example of Delay in action—here too, a simple phrase is used to send a clear message to the person being harassed: I see you; I hear you.

"I was standing the appropriate six feet away from the patron being helped in front of me at my local post office. The woman, white, repeatedly said to the South Asian clerk, 'I don't understand what you are saying.' While the clerk's

English was accented, I had no problem understanding him. At one point the woman said, 'Take off your mask so I can understand you.' The clerk responded that he was required to wear his mask. I was thinking of an appropriate direct intervention when the woman finally paid for the service as requested and left the counter. The first thing I said to the clerk when it was my turn was, 'I understood everything you said.' The woman behind me in line, six feet away, said, 'I did too and I'm hearing impaired.' The woman who had repeated, "I don't understand what you are saying," was still in the service area but she did not say anything. The clerk said she comes in with the same approach each week. He thanked me for telling him he spoke clearly."[66]

They say kindness is contagious—and so is bystander intervention. When you see someone else intervening in a simple but impactful way, like what happened in this story at the post office, you want to join in. The result here was twice the support, twice the impact.

Sometimes Delay requires no words at all.
It can be as simple as a gesture or a knowing glance. These gestures can be especially helpful in situations where you may not speak the same language as the person being harassed.

One day Emily was riding the train with a former intern on the way back from a city council hearing on street harassment when a woman used Delay:

"There was an elderly woman sitting across from us on the train, but other than that the train wasn't crowded. All of a sudden, we notice the woman is trying to get us to scoot down on the bench, away from the door. We look toward the

door to try and figure out why—and that's when we see it:
a man fully exposed, fully erect, touching himself. We both
scream, and the man walks away.

Afterward, we look back over at the woman. She doesn't
say anything, but she just shakes her head in disgust at the
man. It was so small, so simple, but I felt so cared for in that
moment. She knew it wasn't okay, it wasn't our fault. And on
some small level that helped us understand too that it wasn't
okay, and it wasn't our fault."

In another demonstration of a non-verbal form of Delay, our team member Jae Cameron (she/they) was riding the train while in their last trimester of pregnancy. They saw someone being harassed at the other end of the train—and no one was doing anything. Jae decided to get up from their seat, make their way down to the other end of the moving train, and simply sit next to the person being harassed. They didn't say anything. Everyone else on the train saw Jae doing this, and suddenly the bystanders all jumped into action to take care of the individual being harassed and to get the one causing harm off the train. Just by sitting next to that person, Jae encouraged others to take action, too.

In another scenario, a woman saw a young white man yelling at a young Asian woman. She couldn't tell what was going on, only that by the time she could reach her, the man was already walking away:

"There was something in her eyes, she just looked kinda
frozen, so I approached and just said 'Hey, you want a hug?'
and she said 'Yeah,' and once we embraced she was able
to cry it out a little bit. I knew that I am perceived as non-
threatening to most people (I'm a small woman), and that the
specifics of their conflict didn't matter. This person needed

comfort, and I was happy to use the Delay method and offer what I could in that moment."

Knowing yourself, and how you're perceived, can help expand your options to Delay. Pregnant folks and small women are often perceived as less physically threatening, which can make action like a hug, or simply sitting beside someone, feel comforting. But this woman also reminds us of something incredibly important to bystander intervention: You don't need the full story. In fact, you don't need context at all. If you see someone hurting, it's okay to comfort them. The ability to see one another's humanity is what matters.

Sometimes Delay requires watching and waiting.

If something feels "off," it may be. A good strategy can be quietly watching and waiting to gain context. For example, in this next story, the bystander sees a man chatting with a young woman. While this could be consensual, the bystander trusts their instincts and keeps watching. The man then put his arm in the woman's.

> *"I couldn't hear what he was saying, but was keeping an eye out, unsure if I should walk over and check in with her. As soon as he left, she quickly walked over to stand next to me. I asked if she was okay, if she knew the guy. She said 'No, I don't know him. I was just trying to be polite and hoping he didn't get violent.'"* [67]

It's not uncommon for people experiencing harassment to play along in an attempt to try to de-escalate the situation. As a bystander, this can be confusing and can cause you to second guess your instincts. In this instance, the bystander kept watching and, slowly but surely, indicating that they were a safe space. When the young woman came over to stand next to them, they checked in.

CHAPTER EIGHT

Pair Delay with other forms of bystander intervention.

Here's an example of pairing Distract with Delay, as shared by a woman who identified herself as "a small Asian woman in [her] forties":

> *"I felt someone's breath on the left side of my neck. I turned down the volume [of my headphones] and realized a man seated behind me was leaning forward and saying sexually, physically violent, and racist things to me. As I was trying to decide what to do, he got out of his seat and blocked me in my seat while standing over me, and his threats grew even louder, so other folks nearby could hear it, too. There were several people nearby who were watching this happen, including some men, but nobody helped. I would have had to physically push past him in order to get away and was afraid that if I said something back or pushed past him, he would escalate further. I made eye contact with some of the other people on the train, but they all looked away. It was isolating and scary.*
>
> *But then a small young woman in her twenties came from somewhere behind us and loudly said, 'Is someone sitting there?' She pushed past him and asked me to move over so she could sit between us and then started talking to me about random things. She then asked where I was getting off and said she was getting off wherever I was. Her actions made the man move away a couple of feet. He tried to start something with another man, and the second man postured and said, 'Oh, so you want to step to me now? That's a mistake.' He backed away from that guy and just hovered in our vicinity.*

When we got off the train, he didn't follow us. The young
lady then checked in with me on the platform and asked if I
was okay and if there was any other support I needed. I am
still so grateful for her beyond measure and wish I had the
wherewithal at the time to ask her name, but I was still in
shock. I think of her every now and then with gratitude for
how she chose to involve herself in the situation."

This bystander not only started a conversation with the woman, but also took the time to find out where she was getting off and assured her they would exit together. Small actions like these aren't about "making a scene" or "being a hero" or even educating the person doing the harassing. They're about kindness and caring.

Delay can also be paired effectively with Direct. In another story we received, a bystander sees a young woman being sexually harassed and grabbed by a group of men. She directly sets a boundary by saying "leave her alone" (Direct). She then pivots her approach to Delay: "I offered her a ride home if she didn't feel safe or comfortable with walking home, and she kindly accepted. I drove her home and said, 'I'm so sorry that happened to you.'"

It's also worth noting that identity matters here. In both of these stories, the women being harassed likely may have felt less comfortable getting into the bystanders' cars, or being walked home, if the bystanders were men.

Does this mean that as a man you shouldn't offer to help a woman or gender-expansive person get home safely? No, you still should offer if you feel safe doing so, but you should be aware of—and have understanding and sensitivity to—any hesitation that they would have about accepting. If they decline, don't take it personally—after all, they've just been harassed and probably feel very vulnerable. Instead, you could offer to pay for their ride home. Of course, these actions are above and beyond.

Delay can be healing.

The antidote to a world where harassment happens is strengthening community ties. Knowing that your community has your back, and building relationships in your community, can help you feel safer—not to mention happier and healthier. In this next story a Spanish-speaking family moved into a new neighborhood where a white neighbor was upset by the new family's dogs barking, and they began complaining about the noise to another Spanish-speaking neighbor. This neighbor writes:

> *"I asked her if she had let [the new neighbors] know about her concern. She went on to say that she had tried but 'they don't speak any English!' At that moment, a car pulled into the driveway of the new neighbor's home. She immediately went to the parked car and began saying very loudly, 'Dogs barking! All day long! Tell your husband!' She was not speaking in complete sentences and was speaking very loudly in the hope that would make them understand. The young woman driving the car was frozen in fear. She wouldn't get out of the car. . . . I could tell she was very young and was likely a teenager."*

DELAY

This bystander continued to suggest solutions, including Google Translate, but the neighbor "didn't really want the solution. She wanted to complain about the fact that she thought they shouldn't be in our country if they couldn't speak English. She reiterated her concern loudly." Finally, the bystander gave up, and in frustration directly intervened by setting a clear boundary:

> *"'I have to stop you there. What you are saying is hurting me. My family and I speak Spanish. These comments are actually racist. They hurt me.' The neighbor was very taken aback but replied, 'Yes, but you speak ENGLISH!' 'Yes,'*

I replied, 'we do that to make YOU feel comfortable, but we don't have to.'"

This bystander then continues the story:

"I went home horrified that this was the welcome she had had to the neighborhood. I was distraught all evening. Finally, I decided that I couldn't let any more time pass. I frantically began baking cookies. I piled them all on a large plate and told my husband it was time to meet the new neighbors. We calmly walked hand in hand to their house. The neighbor who had made the offensive remarks was in her driveway. We walked past her and knocked on the door of the neighbors. They peeked cautiously through the curtains, visibly nervous to open the door. Finally, they came to the door and spoke ENGLISH to us! We began speaking Spanish. I shared what had happened earlier that day and asked for the young woman driving the car that afternoon. She was their sixteen-year-old daughter. I told her that I baked the cookies to welcome them to the neighborhood. I told her that she should never have to experience that in this country, and if she had any further issues, she should let me know. She was very grateful, and the family are now friends of ours. I walked home that night, holding my husband's hand, feeling proud that I spoke up for what was right. I will never stay silent again."

By delaying, checking in on the family afterward, and bringing them cookies, this bystander not only supported the family in feeling safer and welcomed in their new community, but also made new friends—which is likely to make the *bystander* feel safer and more at home, too. In the

People who experience harassment can be racist, too.

After training at a local community college in New York City, a young Black man came up to Emily and asked, "If there is an assumption that men of color are sexual predators, should I try to intervene at all? Won't I just scare the person being harassed?" Here's the thing: Identity is complicated. If you're a man, be aware of your privilege. If you're Black, don't let the racism that society throws on you stop you from being your best self. If the people on behalf of whom you're intervening can't see your support as the goodwill it's intended to be, know that isn't your fault or responsibility.

That said, always remember to assess your own safety before attempting any form of intervention, even Delay. Black folks and other folks of color will also need to assess how likely this person is to call the police on them. There is a history of racist people turning the police onto people of color without cause (remember the story of Amy Cooper and Christian Cooper?), and an equally long history of the police turning violent against people of color for small or nonexistent infractions. Take for example Philando Castile, a Black man who was pulled over at a routine traffic stop and was shot to death in front of his family.[68]

As a bystander, it's critical that you trust your instincts and take care of your own safety first. If you're concerned that Delay might be misperceived, consider another intervention like Delegate.

long-term, gestures like these remind us that bystander intervention isn't exclusively about responding to harassment in the moment, it is also about building the world we want to live in.

What to avoid when you Delay.

When you Delay, it's key to make sure you never:

- Tell the person who was harassed what they should have or could have done differently to avoid the harassment.

- Give the person advice on what they should do next unless they explicitly ask.

- Try to minimize the harassment or otherwise imply that "it's not a big deal."

While Delay is so simple on its surface, it can and does go wrong. Take, for example, this story of a person who was spat on while commuting to work:

> *"When I got to work, I told a coworker, a dude, about being spit on, and his reaction was along the lines of, 'Well that's New York for you.'*
>
> *If it hadn't been for someone else's perceptive and kind father seeing me and offering to hold space for me, to simply be with me, I may not have ever acknowledged how much this incident affected me, even to myself. I think of the Delayer every once in a while. I hope his daughters know how much comfort and recognition he brought to me when I didn't know I needed it, and I hope that he or someone else intervenes for them if they ever need it."*

In contrast to the coworker's dismissive response—where he missed an opportunity to offer kindness and affirm that the harassment was undeserved—the Delayer in this story offered to "hold space for me, to simply be with me." When done well, it's a simple gesture, but a powerful and memorable one nonetheless.

DELAY AT WORK

At work, Delay is that conversation by the coffee pot afterward. It's that mid-meeting-bathroom-break-turned-WTF-just-happened debrief. As in a public space, it's the check-in. But unlike in public space, these are people with whom you have established relationships. There are differences in power to consider. There are ongoing dynamics to be mitigated. There is HR and its investigations. At work, Delay follows the same approach, but it has different pitfalls.

How to Delay in Virtual Meetings

As the world and the workplace increasingly moves online and remote work becomes the norm, Delay becomes one of the most useful tactics in the workplace because it's easy to touch base with people one-on-one in a virtual environment.

Here's an example: Emily was on a call with a funder, trying to adapt a bystander intervention curriculum to work in Brazil, with the guidance and expertise of a local Brazilian organization. The funder, who was not born in Brazil, repeatedly referred to the cultural adaptation as "tropicalizing" the curriculum. Emily had never done work in Brazil and didn't know the customs or terminology, but it just didn't sound right to her. Emily DM'd the leader of the local organization over Zoom and asked, "Do you use the term 'tropicalize' the curriculum? It sounds racist." The leader of the local organization responded "TOTALLY RACIST," in all-caps. By then the call was almost over, but at the very minimum, Emily knew not to repeat the racist language. She then sent a follow-up email to check in on the local partners after the call.

On the "no response" response.

Many bystanders are dubious about whether or not Delay has a meaningful impact—or question if "bringing it up again makes it worse." This next story is told by someone who didn't have anyone do anything on her behalf:

"Very early in my career, while at work, a guest was on a tour of the office. He stopped at my desk and asked me lots of non-work-related questions (most of which I don't remember). He ended our conversation by calling me 'almond eyes.'

Being only eighteen years old, I lacked the tools and confidence to respond. I felt embarrassed that it happened and only later realized that others in the room either didn't see it happen, or worse, intentionally ignored the interaction.

Even a knowing glance (something I learned in Bystander Training!) would have made all the difference in how I felt the weeks, months, and years following. No action is too small from an ally."

Time and time again, we hear that when no one does anything, it makes the situation worse.

Giving the Power Back

Using Delay at work is an opportunity to put the person being harassed back in control. Some people will want to report the harassment to HR, and they will need backup and a witness to what happened. Others will feel a sense of shame and will want you to tell no one. (Remember: even if they don't specifically request that you tell no one, other people's harassment stories are never yours to share without their permission.)

No matter where someone is in processing their experience of harassment, Delay is not about convincing them to be somewhere else or influencing their subsequent actions. Your job is simply to support them exactly how they say they would like to be supported, regardless of whether you agree or disagree with their decisions around their experience.

DELAY ONLINE

When it comes to in-person harassment, we know from our research with Cornell University that as little as a knowing glance can reduce the trauma related to harassment. It's not much different online, if you replace a knowing glance with a DM or text.

Delay online is still a simple check-in.

But instead of asking if they need a ride home, it's asking if they need help reporting the harassment or tightening up their digital security. While this may seem obvious, too often we see that this step has been missed in the process. One bystander who often intervenes on behalf of their friend shared with us:

"I rarely see it in real-time, but when I do notice a particular swelling of harassment, I make it a point to send him a text message or DM that articulates my gratitude for his work and affirms that the folks saying terrible things are, in fact, terrible. He does a lot of work to demonstrate and document instances of harassment as points of education for the folks who follow him, but he never deserves the vitriol he gets from so many directions. I know he appreciates connections from people who know him offline as a way to keep his work grounded in the relationships and love that nourish him."

Most people who experience harassment understand that not everyone in the world is going to be kind to or agree with them. But what's a little harder to stomach is that one can be publicly humiliated. What we see time and time again is that the trauma associated with others observing harassment but not offering any form of support is oftentimes worse than the trauma of the original incident.

Anonymous supportive messages work, too.

On Right To Be's website, people who submit their stories of online harassment can ask our vetted community of bystanders to send them supportive messages when they are facing online harassment. One of our users writes:

"Receiving messages of support from people was a form of relief. It reminded me that there are people who care enough about what is going on to write to me about it at a time when I felt upset and very isolated. They also countered the negativity and ensured that there was a stream of online positivity coming my way, which helped make the digital space feel safer again."

Anonymous, supportive messages like these can help mitigate the pain of online harassment. Online harassment hurts so deeply because it's often anonymous. You're not sure how many of them there are or how angry they are. It's easy to imagine that there are hundreds out there plotting your death (and to be sure, this can happen). The "not knowing" can infiltrate how you see the world. When Emily was experiencing a lot of anonymous online harassment, everything started to feel unsafe. Even the person who sold her coffee, or the man standing next to her in line, would make her wonder, "Is that person secretly harassing me online, too?"

While supportive messages don't fix everything, they do offer a sense of greater balance. It creates a different story if the person selling you coffee or standing next to you in line could also be the person sending you anonymous supportive messages, that you're strong, and that they are here to help. The world doesn't start to feel safe, exactly, but receiving support can reframe the mental narrative that it is wholly unsafe.

A supportive message is simple. A text. A quick note. A GIF, or maybe a little gift. But the impact is significant. It validates the experience of the person being harassed: "Yes, that is harassment. No, that's not okay." In doing so, it can reduce trauma and support healing.

LAST WORDS ON DELAY

We all want someone to care when we're faced with hate and harassment. Harassment is meant to erase our humanity. But when it happens, we shouldn't be charged with redrawing the contours of our life all by ourselves. We are social animals—we need each other to love, to grow, and to heal. When you Delay, you're not stopping the harassment, but you may in fact be able to stop the bleeding. And that's the first step toward healing.

DIRECT

It's the only one of the 5Ds that involves directly confronting the person doing the harassing—which means it's the biggest safety risk. But Direct isn't about strapping on superhero spandex, swooping in, and saving the day. In fact, it's not about heroics at all. Like all the other forms of bystander intervention, it's about prioritizing the person being harassed; only this time, before turning your attention to them, you're clearly but firmly setting a boundary with the person doing the harassing.

We choose to discuss Direct last because people tend to assume that directly intervening when they witness harassment or disrespectful behavior is the only option—and that sometimes causes them to freeze. This is especially true if they see violent behavior or abuse happening. In some of the stories we share in this chapter, you'll see that choosing Direct could put the bystander at an increased risk of being targeted. In general, people of any marginalized identity share that kind of risk.

Another key point to remember is that while it is important to speak out about harassment, as bystanders we always want to make sure that we are centering the person experiencing it— and their needs. If you witness someone who's being harassed already speaking up for themselves and creating a boundary, you don't need to directly intervene in a way where you end up speaking over them. Instead, stand with them silently in solidarity, or back up what they say with a simple statement like, "They've told you to leave them alone, and I am here to support them," or, "I agree that was an inappropriate comment."

DIRECT IN PUBLIC

The most important consideration when using Direct in public spaces is safety. Ultimately, as well intentioned as you may be, you can't help someone else find safety by entering a situation where your own safety is at risk. Before intervening, listen to your gut instinct, assess your surroundings and the situation, and then decide if Direct is the right option for you.

Assess your safety.

We recommend using Right To Be's Pyramid of Escalation to evaluate a situation of harassment you witness. The Pyramid of Escalation is a visual model of what conflict can look like at different stages of intensity. Here on the Pyramid of Escalation, you can see three levels: agitation, escalation, and peak conflict.

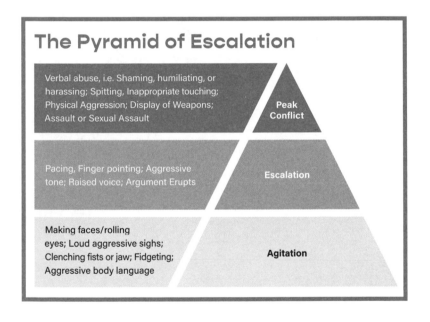

The Pyramid of Escalation

Verbal abuse, i.e. Shaming, humiliating, or harassing; Spitting, Inappropriate touching; Physical Aggression; Display of Weapons; Assault or Sexual Assault

Peak Conflict

Pacing, Finger pointing; Aggressive tone; Raised voice; Argument Erupts

Escalation

Making faces/rolling eyes; Loud aggressive sighs; Clenching fists or jaw; Fidgeting; Aggressive body language

Agitation

Some questions you should consider when prioritizing your safety are:

- **Where on this pyramid is the person doing the harassing?** Before proceeding in any situation of conflict, ask yourself: Am I comfortable engaging with someone who is already agitated, especially if I don't know them? It's okay if the answer is no. Know your limits. However, while making your assessment, it's important to remember that certain behaviors listed under "Agitation" here can sometimes be the result of neurodivergence—for example, autism. These situations don't require conflict intervention, but if you make a mistake in assessing the situation, know that none of the forms of bystander intervention we teach you will cause harm.

- **Where am I on this pyramid?** While this may seem like a funny question to ask, you're not alone if harassment pisses you off. (Just look at us, we're so pissed off we wrote a whole book!) You're also not alone if witnessing the harassment of others activates memories of your own experiences. The trick is first to de-escalate yourself. If you're escalated, chances are your energy will be perceived, matched, or worse, exceeded. De-escalation strategies include breath-regulating exercises like box breathing (inhale for four seconds, pause for four, exhale for four, pause for four, and repeat) or grounding exercises like putting your feet on the floor, your back against the back of your chair (if you're in one), and naming in your head three things you see, two things you can touch, and one thing you can hear. If you're unable to return to a calm state at that moment, you may want to pick an indirect form of intervention to avoid escalating the situation.

- **Can your identities put you at increased risk?** If you're witnessing anti-trans harassment and you're trans identified, you might not feel safe intervening directly. That's okay—there are other options. Don't beat yourself up for not being able to intervene in the way you want to most—instead, honor your instinct for self-care and prioritizing your safety.

- **Are your own biases affecting how you perceive the situation?** Many people look at this one and think, "But I'm not biased! I'm intervening against bias!" Here's the cold, hard truth: We all hold implicit bias. The best way to deal with it is to be consciously aware of our bias and manage against it. For example, if you see a situation that looks as if a Black man is harassing someone, acknowledge the racial stereotype of the "aggressive Black man" and perhaps ask yourself, "Would I feel as threatened if they were a white woman?" We also hold bias on who, or what, is safe.

DIRECT

- **Can you access the exits?** Familiarity with the venue in which the situation is happening can increase your sense of safety and help you make sure you can reach a safer place quickly if things escalate.

- **Are you with people who have your back?** Bystander intervention works best when there are other bystanders present to support, even if their only job is to look out for you, the person intervening directly. Maybe it's your best friend who is with you, or maybe you've had a chance to briefly make eye contact with a stranger who looks as concerned about the situation as you do. Checking in explicitly before you take action can help ensure support.

While your first instinct might be Direct, it may not actually be in the best interest of you or others. You might also discover that you're perfectly positioned to act directly. No matter what you decide, it's important to remember that the priority is the person being harassed. It's not your job (nor is it helpful) to educate someone who is harassing or prove them wrong. It is your job to make sure the person being harassed feels cared for. So avoid the back and forth of a moral debate with the person harassing, as tempting as that can be.

What do you do if they respond?

Once you intervene, the person harassing might try to engage you by making inflammatory remarks. Ignore them. Do not give them more attention than they deserve. Here's why: Arguing with the person harassing can put the person you were trying to help at an increased risk. Now, instead of having one escalated person on their hands, they have two, and that can make them feel even more vulnerable, afraid, or alone.

During Jorge's first couple weeks at Right To Be, he learned the power of Direct, but also that sometimes it's not enough on its own. One day he went downstairs to the mailroom of the Right To Be office. While walking into the mailroom, he heard a male voice cursing and yelling racist comments. As he got closer to our mailbox, he heard a woman saying, "Please leave me alone." Immediately, he walked up to the woman to check in and ask her if she was okay. Right then, the man hurled another insult at the woman. Jorge firmly told the man, "That is inappropriate and racist. She asked you to leave her alone; please walk away and stop talking to her."

Typically, this has worked in the past, as Jorge recognizes some of the privileges he holds as a six-foot-tall, 350-pound male. But this day it did not, and instead of walking away, the man then began to insult Jorge.

Jorge instantly got angry and prepared himself to verbally spar with this man, but then he glanced down and was faced with a look of terror on the woman's face. It was a complete contrast to the look of relief she'd had when Jorge had stepped up to say something about the disrespectful behavior. It clicked in his mind that the woman was afraid that Jorge was about to escalate the situation further. So, he grounded himself and realized that he needed to find another way to intervene. He ended up choosing Delegate and finding the building's security personnel. The security guard knew both Jorge and the woman personally, so Jorge felt comfortable he would handle it well. A few days later, the woman came to our office to thank Jorge for intervening.

Jorge realized that while Direct was his Superpower and it had worked in the past, this situation was complex. In this case, an elderly white man was harassing an Asian woman. When Jorge stepped in, he was at an increased risk because of his identity and presentation as an Afro-Latinx individual—so when the man saw Jorge, he immediately began to use the same racist approach. This story illustrates just how much your identity matters and has the potential to put you at an increased risk.

Being direct with the police.

Your racial identity is also an important thing to consider when dealing with the police, due to a historical record of high rates of police violence toward communities of color in many countries around the globe. In this next story, a thirteen-year-old Black girl was with her mom and two little siblings when they were pulled over by a white, male officer for "not stopping at the stop sign correctly." She writes:

"My mom was very polite, but not overly deferential. . . . My mom had instructed us in advance to only provide our name and basic profile information to the police and to defer all

questions to the adults. I politely told him my name, how to spell it, my birthday, and my age, and referred him to my mom for any other questions. . . .

He was not satisfied with that encounter. He got angry and returned back to my mom's side of the car and asked her to exit the vehicle and then handcuffed her for no reason. My youngest sister got very upset and started yelling and crying. I ended up having to hold her on my lap to calm her down.

He came back over to my side of the car and started asking me a bunch of questions, but I was just a kid, and I was scared that he'd handcuffed her and no one was around, so I stuck to my mom's instructions. He then lowered his voice and said to me that I'd better start answering his questions or he was going to take us away from our mom and make sure we kids would be separated from her and put into separate foster homes. Internally I was really upset, but externally, as the eldest sibling, I did not waver from my polite, standard responses.

Someone in the neighborhood passed by and saw what was going on and shouted out at the cop to ask why the heck he handcuffed my mom and what he was doing to us kids. More people started to gather and question the situation. He eventually uncuffed my mom and left without giving her a ticket or anything. We thanked folks in the neighborhood and went on our way home, which was just down the street."

Here, the action of others de-escalated what could have become an even more traumatic situation. But it was also a risk. Directly intervening with police can escalate quickly, especially for marginalized groups. If you don't feel comfortable directly intervening with the police, this may be a situation where you choose to Document or Delegate to someone less likely to be targeted by police (like white folks).

And yet, in this situation, it worked. Once someone in the neighborhood intervened, others joined in. And once there were multiple witnesses, it showed the police officer that he wasn't going to get away with this abuse of power. When we see other people intervening, we have a natural inclination to intervene, too.

Set a clear boundary.

Sometimes, the best thing you can do is to be clear about what's wrong and what's happening next. In this story, submitted by a singer and musician, his friend who witnessed his harassment didn't get into a back-and-forth—they simply set a boundary:

"Two years ago, I found myself in a different country. This destination was known for being very queer-friendly, so I could have never expected what would happen next. While walking down an isolated path with two friends, three men on motorbikes circled us. They were displaying crude gestures and shouted offensive language to mock the queer community. Then, they stopped in front of us to ask me about my gender identity. I didn't know how to respond, but luckily, I didn't have to.

My friend felt comfortable enough to say, 'Why do you have to be so rude? We're having a great night, don't be that way.' Finally, one of the other men on the bikes hurried his friend

off and the three left us. My friends then asked if I was okay and shared that they loved me the way I am. Although I was still shocked, I was so thankful that I had friends who protected me and stood up for me. To this day, I am grateful that even in this jarring situation, I learned that the best thing we can do is support each other, especially when confronted with hate."

After boundaries were set, the friend turned their attention back to the person being harassed. The intervention didn't involve educating the three men or even asking them further questions. It was just about doing the next right thing—taking care of the person being harassed.

DIRECT AT WORK

At this point, you may wonder how to use Direct in a work setting without being confrontational or accusatory.

The answer is that using Direct can be complicated and feel uncomfortable in a work setting where maintaining relationships is important and specific power dynamics are at play. You might wonder how this will work with your boss. Or, if you're a manager, you may often feel pressure to use Direct just because you are "in charge," even if it's not your preferred method of bystander intervention. These are valid concerns. The good news is that to use Direct, you don't always have to be confrontational.

Deploy Direct as a clarifying question.

Meetings and other group settings are a common environment for disrespect or microaggressions in the workplace. Let's say you're at a brainstorming session and Jenny has a brilliant idea. No one acknowledges it, and the meeting proceeds. Later, Sandy says the same thing and is praised for the idea—and no one makes any effort to attribute the idea back to Jenny. These things happen, sometimes by accident. But because sexism, racism, and more biases are alive and well in workplaces, these things disproportionately happen to marginalized folks.

Still, it's hard as a bystander to blatantly say "That's racist!" But this doesn't mean you shouldn't intervene. Try a gentle form of Direct, like asking a question: "Didn't Jenny have that idea earlier?" Then make eye contact with Jenny to encourage her to chime in. Afterward, you can check in with Jenny and let her decide if further action is needed, or if she just wants to grab a coffee with you to vent.

Asking people a clarifying question can give them the opportunity to rethink what they've just said and ideally catch their mistake. Sometimes that might not happen right away, but a clarifying question still helps. Here's another example: Jaleesa, an Afro-Latina school social worker, works at a school that serves predominantly Black and Latinx students but has a predominantly white staff. During a weekly staff Zoom meeting, she shared a status update about her meetings with her students in which she noted that many of them were consistently late to their sessions and that she wanted to come up with a solution. One of the teachers commented, "Well, you know those kids are always late. It's how they are; those people are always late."

Jaleesa was taken aback by the comment and responded with a clarifying question: "What do you mean by 'those kids and those people are always late?'" The teacher laughed nervously and responded, "I'm just saying, you know what I mean." Jaleesa then asked an even more straightforward question: "I'm not sure I understand what you mean. Are you referring to the fact that my students are Black and brown? Please elaborate, because I am not sure what you mean." After an awkward silence and some discomfort, the meeting continued—but toward the end, the teacher publicly acknowledged that she had realized her comment was inappropriate and apologized.

Jaleesa's story is a great example of how a clarifying question can require a followup question. If, for instance, you see someone else intervening in workplace harassment by asking a clarifying question, back them up by adding something simple, like, "Yeah, what did you mean?" or, "I was confused by that, too."

Set a gentle-but-firm boundary at work.

There are situations where a clarifying question isn't the right response. Let's say you are facilitating a meeting and one person is talking over everyone else and derailing the meeting. You can simply say, "Thank you for sharing, but I'd like to give the rest of the team an opportunity to share their thoughts." It's not rude and sets a boundary that allows others to participate in the conversation, too.

The customer isn't always right.

You could also witness disrespect or harassment perpetrated by a client or customer, which can be difficult to navigate—especially in a culture that takes "the customer is always right" as a truism. That's not always the case, and when customers or clients disrespect employees, it is important to show up in support of your team members, taking the stance that disrespectful behavior in the workplace is not tolerated.

One person shared with us an example from their workplace and explained how they successfully intervened using Direct:

> *"I was working in an office setting at the reception desk where there were usually two to three employees to greet customers and offer help. One of my coworkers is from Puerto Rico and speaks perfect English with a bit of an accent.*
>
> *One day a customer came in and did not want her to help him. He became belligerent, and I stepped in and told him that he was not behaving in a manner acceptable for our office and that she was the best person to help him from among those at the reception desk area, as she also had the most experience and knowledge. He reluctantly calmed down some and accepted her help, but it was a very disconcerting incident."*

As a business owner, it can be hard to set these boundaries. But it's important—not just in an effort to care for your employees, but also to care for your customers. If your customers see harassment happening at your business, it will make them feel less safe, even if it doesn't happen to them directly. By intervening, you're setting the norm that harassment isn't okay. This can help to recover a sense of safety for staff and customers alike.

Here's a great example of a manager having their employee's back while dealing with an abusive customer:

> *"Many years ago (the nineties), I was the manager of a sandwich shop. One of my fellow employees/friends was transitioning from female to male at the time. . . . He is very kind and personable and was well-liked by fellow staff and customers. And made great sandwiches!*
>
> *One day, a woman who I did not recognize came in and publicly berated him for his appearance, saying that he shouldn't be allowed to work directly with customers. We all were horrified, and my friend was in tears. I told the woman she had to leave and not to return unless she apologized. She threatened to call and did call the owner of the store to complain about us and insist that we be fired; him for his appearance and me for telling her to leave.*
>
> *The owner, bless his heart, told the woman because of her behavior, she was not welcome in the store, and that we were valued employees.*
>
> *My friend was quite traumatized/embarrassed by the incident at the time, but I think the support from the owner of the store [and] his fellow employees helped immensely."*

Here, you see the support escalate. When the manager set a boundary, the store owner set a boundary as well. Gestures like this on behalf of management are better for business than the sale of a couple extra sandwiches, because they support a feeling of emotional safety at work among your team.

Set norms as a manager.

The best thing about Direct in the workplace is that it sets a clear norm. This is part of the reason that managers feel pressure to be Direct, but it's important to recognize that not every manager is well-suited for Direct intervention. If you're a manager who doesn't feel comfortable responding directly in the moment, you can always work to set a norm after the fact. You might consider:

- Bringing it up at the next staff meeting and setting a clear expectation around the behavior you witnessed.

- Sending out an email clarifying expectations afterward.

- Signing your team up for training on respect in the workplace, harassment, microaggressions, and/or implicit bias, depending on what happened.

- Reporting what happened, if it was harassment or discrimination—even if you think it was insignificant or just a joke. As a manager, you have a duty to report harassment to Human Resources (or if you don't have HR, your boss—or if you don't have a boss, your board). If your boss is the one doing the harassing, you'll need to jump to their boss (or the organization's board, if they are the CEO).

As a manager, you should also Delay and have a conversation with the recipient of the harassment and/or disrespect to learn what next steps they would like. While you can't guarantee that you'll be able to meet their demands, some next steps like extending deadlines, moving desks, or a mediated conversation may be possible. You should also meet with the person who did the action to set a clear boundary and avoid repeat incidents. While these are obvious next steps, these alone don't work to set an effective norm in a workplace, and your team can still feel unprotected, as harassment happening to one member of the team can leave the rest of the team feeling vulnerable and unsafe.

DIRECT ONLINE

If you're going to directly intervene online, it's best to secure your digital safety first. Here are some simple steps that you should take. These are good practices in general, but they are essential if you decide to intervene.

STEP ONE: Secure your accounts.

Here are two easy ways to do so:

- **Set up two-step verification.** Two-step verification is an additional layer of security to prevent others from accessing your accounts on social media or other online services. When you activate this extra authentication, you will receive a code via SMS that you'll need to enter whenever you or someone else tries to log in to your account from an unfamiliar browser or computer.

- **Make your passwords stronger.** Use a different password for each platform, and keep in mind that a strong password is around ten characters or more and includes uppercase letters, lowercase letters, numbers, and symbols. Don't put your passwords in your cloud (i.e., Google Drive, Dropbox, or iCloud) in case it gets hacked. Instead, consider using an online password manager, such as LastPass, that creates and keeps track of highly random, high-security passwords for every account you access online, and even suggests secure passwords for you.

STEP TWO: De-dox yourself.

Doxing occurs when someone publishes another person's private or identifying information on the internet, such as their home address, phone number, or social security number. It is a tactic used to make individuals feel unsafe, extort them, or make them vulnerable to other forms of harassment both online and in person, such as stalking.

Check the following websites to find out if your personal information is posted publicly and then submit a request to get it removed. Set a reminder to check again every six months. These sites "scrape" data off publicly available documents, sell it for a premium, and repopulate themselves regularly. We know, it's creepy!

- Spokeo (to remove listing: http://www.spokeo.com/opt_out/new)

- Anywho.com (to remove listing: https://www.intelius.com/opt-out/submit/)

- Whitepages (to remove listing: https://www.whitepages.com/suppression-requests)

There are hundreds of other websites just like these, but this is a good place to start. Many countries have outlawed sites like this, but in the United States, they unfortunately persist unregulated.

STEP THREE: Avoid sharing identifying information online.

Never share your phone number or address online, and avoid sharing details on social media like where you live or where you like to hang out. Also, be careful about posting information that can be used to figure out the answers to your security questions, such as the name of a childhood pet or other names you have been known by.

STEP FOUR: Do not open links or attachments from an unknown or suspicious account.

Clicking unverified links or downloading an attachment from an unknown source might expose you to malware. In a scam known as phishing, cyber-criminals impersonate legitimate organizations or services in order to steal personal information like your passwords or credit card information. For example, you could receive an email in which cybercriminals imper-sonate Instagram, claiming that your account will be banned or removed if you don't enter your username and password. To avoid being scammed, always verify the sender and go to the official website rather than clicking unverified links.

STEP FIVE: Update your devices and use antivirus protection.

When manufacturers launch regular device updates, they usually fix vul-nerabilities or bugs that can be used to access your devices or personal information. Also, antivirus software will alert you of any attempt to install malicious software on your device.

STEP SIX: Cover your camera.

This one is creepy, but if Mark Zuckerberg covers his camera (he does), you should cover yours, too. Hackers can gain access to your camera if you click illegitimate links that hide malware or malicious code in your operating system. If that happens, your system may also end up with more vulnerabilities or bugs that can be exploited by cybercriminals.[69]

Once you've taken these steps to ensure your own safety online, you're ready to consider direct intervention against harassment. Of course, as always, if you decide to intervene, keep in mind that your goal is to support the person being harassed—and not to name, shame, and blast the person doing the harassing off the internet (as tempting as that may be).

Chime In with supportive, affirming, or constructive comments, messages, or hashtags.

This approach is similar to Delay, but with a distinction—with Direct, you are giving all this love in public for anyone (even the people doing the harassing) to read. An example of this is how we saw people intervening to support Leslie Jones with the hashtag #LoveforLeslieJ. Not everyone has the fanbase of Leslie Jones, but every supportive comment helps. In fact, when people share their story of online harassment with Right To Be, supportive messages are the most requested form of support. They validate the person's experience as online harassment and remind them that they didn't deserve it and that there are people in the world who have their back.

While Right To Be allows supportive comments on a private platform, providing such comments on the same platform where the harassment is occurring is also a form of Direct intervention. For example, in response to witnessing harassment of Chelsea Manning on Twitter, @lizzieistrash tweeted, "Chelsea is an immortal goddess, she has little time for petty behavior in her quest for justice and fabulousness #wegotthis," with a string of emojis. This form of Direct isn't about setting a firm boundary, i.e., "You're wrong, leave her alone," but it is a way of speaking out against harassment by offering a counternarrative (this is often referred to as counterspeech). When writer and founder of The UnSlut Project, Emily Lindin,

DIRECT

6 NEW MESSAGES
YOU RULE! <3
I SUPPORT YOU! ☺

heard from a group of students experiencing significant online harassment after sharing accounts of their sexual assaults, she encouraged her followers to flood the hashtag being used to harass them, #OKGirls, with supportive comments about the survivors. Then Lindin documented all the positive tweets (and weeded out the hateful ones) and used Storify to share them with the survivors, so they could see the love without having to witness the harassment.[70]

Fact-check claims or expose impersonation.

This is another way to directly intervene in online harassment. For example, if your friend is being impersonated, you may want to publicly share something like this to show support: "If you're as big a fan of Victoria V as I am, be sure to follow their REAL handle: @victoriav23. Abusive trolls are impersonating them—help me report this impersonation account @vvv23." You're not only elevating Victoria's voice by encouraging others to follow them, you're also getting more people to report the fake accounts in hopes that social media platforms will address the issue quicker and more seriously.

A great example of fact-checking false claims comes from developer Chloe Condon. A man said that Condon had been following him around at a conference; he wrote alongside a photo of Condon, "If I end up missing tonight, tell the police to find this woman. Lol. Has not stopped following me around, asking me questions and telling me about her life since I got off the stage this evening." He ended the post with a string of hashtags including #stalker and #ConferenceSpeakerProblems.

Condon responded by fact-checking the man, saying "I have no idea who you are, nor was I at a conference/meet-up/event w/ you 4 days ago." She added, "photo is from my @NewCo article I published years ago/ from a conference 3 years ago." Condon's online community chimed in and found evidence of this guy harassing others in the past. In response to the rise of negative attention, he abruptly changed his handle and claimed that his Instagram had been hacked. At that point, Condon fact-checked him again by posting, "You changed your Instagram handle last night, so I think you've known about me before this morning."[71]

Direct intervention on an institutional level.

In March 2021, the *New York Times* called out Tucker Carlson for a segment in which he mocked and attacked one of its tech reporters, Taylor Lorenz. Here is the tweet, written by Lorenz, that started the exchange:

"For international women's day please consider supporting women enduring online harassment. It's not an exaggeration to say that the harassment and smear campaign I've had to endure over the past year has destroyed my life. No one should have to go through this."

Carlson made the Twitter post a focus of a segment in which he said:

"Lots of people are suffering right now, but no one is suffering quite as much as Taylor Lorenz is suffering. People have criticized her opinions on the Internet, and it has destroyed her life. Let's pause on this International Women's Day and recognize that. You thought female Uyghurs had it bad. You haven't talked to Taylor Lorenz."[72]

The chyron during the segment read "Society's biggest victims have powerful jobs."

In response, the *New York Times* stated:

"In a now familiar move, Tucker Carlson opened his show last night by attacking a journalist. It was a calculated and cruel tactic, which he regularly deploys to unleash a wave of harassment and vitriol at his intended target. Taylor Lorenz is a talented New York Times *journalist doing timely and essential reporting. Journalists should be able to do their jobs without facing harassment."[73]*

CHAPTER NINE

Intervening as an employer or an institution is a powerful move. It lends credibility to the individual experiencing harassment, and the *New York Times* was able to intervene with little risk to the safety of the rest of its team—institutions have infrastructure in place to manage security that individuals rarely do.

Name the harm.

You don't have to be an institution to call out what you see. In this same case, Laura Olin (@lauraolin), a digital strategist, retweeted a story about the harassment of Taylor Lorenz by Tucker Carlson and called it what it is: "This is targeted abuse. Intent to cause harm."

By retweeting a news story about the harassment without tagging Tucker Carlson, Olin is able to publicly set the norm that harassment is not acceptable while simultaneously minimizing (but not eliminating, since her tweet was still public) the risk of retaliation from Carlson or his followers. Publicly stating what is and isn't acceptable creates norms online while enabling others at risk for the same harassment to feel more seen, heard, and cared for. For example, publicly stating something like, "This is a blatant attempt to use abusive tactics to intimidate and censor a Black reporter, whose talent and skill we need more than ever. Reject hate," can be effective both at setting expectations around what is appropriate when it comes to interacting with others online, and at building awareness of the extent to which both journalists and Black people are disproportionately targeted by online harassment.

LAST WORDS ON DIRECT
Direct intervention gives you an opportunity to set a boundary and create a norm that harassment isn't acceptable. It's a great option, but that doesn't mean it's always the best option. Assess your safety and the safety of the person being harassed, determine the risk of retaliation in the workplace, and/or lock down your digital security before you attempt direct intervention online. And when in doubt, choose another of the 5Ds.

HOW TO MANAGE TRAUMA & BUILD RESILIENCE

It's likely that you're here, dear reader, because you've been treated as "less than" at some point during your life—just for being exactly who you are. When it comes to bystander intervention, your experience is an asset that makes you uniquely equipped to intervene. You intuitively understand the long-term effects of harassment, and if you share the same identities as the person being harassed, it can be easier for you to quickly spot harassment.

It also means that you need to take care of your own well-being. Witnessing harassment can create its own psychological trauma and bring up a lot of buried memories. In this next chapter, we'll talk about how we can manage our own trauma while intervening, and how to build the resilience necessary to heal.

THE IMPACT OF HARASSMENT ON THE BYSTANDER

Just because we didn't experience the harassment directly, doesn't mean that it doesn't harm us. Witnessing harassment can take an emotional toll.

Let's take a look at this study from 2004: Researchers Gregory R. Janson and Richard J. Hazler compared the rates of psychological distress between bystanders who *witnessed* repeated incidents of harassment (but did not necessarily take action) and those who *directly experienced* repeated incidents of harassment.[74] They found that in the moment of the harassment, the person being harassed was in more distress than the bystander who witnessed it—but after that moment passed, their distress levels were "not significantly different." The study showed that the long-term effects of repeated harassment are very similar for both the person who experienced it and the person who witnessed it.

This can feel like a radical conclusion, but when we start to think about our own experiences witnessing harassment and the ways in which that experience can stick with us, it makes more sense.

Recent neuroscience research has discovered special types of neurons called "mirror neurons."[75] While most of our neurons focus on incoming sensory input and on outgoing motor commands to our muscles, "mirror neurons" go a step further.[76] According to neuroscientist Vilayanur Ramachandran, "mirror neurons," or "empathy neurons," fire in your brain when you witness someone else taking an action or being touched, almost as if you were the person taking action or being touched. The only reason you know you're not is because your touch and pain receptors tell your brain that you're not. Cool, huh?

Ramachandran explains further in his famous TED talk: If your arm is completely numb, and you watch someone else being touched on the hand, you can literally feel that touch in your hand that's otherwise numb. He says, "All that's separating you from [the person being touched] is your skin. Remove the skin, you experience that person's touch in your mind. You've dissolved the barrier between you and other human beings."

The idea that we are all connected is a shared foundation of many faiths and philosophical traditions, but as Ramachandran points out, mirror neurons show us our interconnectedness goes beyond philosophy; it's biology, too. Our brains use mirror neurons to dissolve the divide between "your trauma" and "my trauma," and what results is "our trauma." So if you're feeling the pain of someone else's experience of harassment, there is nothing wrong with you and you're not "overreacting." Feeling the pain of others is a very human response.

OUR BODIES HOLD TRUTHS

Our bodies hold truths that our minds aren't ready for yet. Our bodies hold our history. Somatics coach Madeline Wade says, "Our body is stories, narrative, emotions, and energy."

In *The Mindbody Prescription*, John E. Sarno demonstrates that when we don't make adequate space in our lives for our emotional pain, the body can get creative and begin to express its emotional pain as physical pain—from ulcers to back pain to autoimmune disorders. The brain can even play a trick where it withholds adequate oxygen from a part of our body in order to create pain where there otherwise is no physical problem. The pain in these cases is very real, to be sure—the root cause, though, is not a physical, bodily issue, but rather the insufficient care of our emotional well-being.

And while some traumas happen during our lives, others are inherited from generations past. Enslavement, war, genocide, abuse, and other life-changing events faced by our ancestors can lead to what is known as "generational trauma."

Our ancestors' trauma is quite literally written into our genes. As Resmaa Menakem points out in *My Grandmother's Hands: Racialized Trauma and the Pathway to Mending our Hearts and Bodies*, psychological trauma has the potential to alter the epigenetic makeup of future generations.[77] The mark doesn't directly mutate the gene. Instead, it alters the mechanism by which the gene expresses itself.

These chemical marks are passed down from generation to generation. They shape how we respond to the inevitable traumas in our own lives. "No one has a perfect childhood," says Madeline Wade. "If a trauma is repressed and not given room to heal, trauma can start to leak out in our bodies, our minds, and our actions." If managed well, trauma can provide a springboard for us to learn, grow, and heal throughout our lifetime.[78]

BUILDING OUR RESILIENCE

In the same way that our traumas are shared when they are witnessed, so is our resilience and healing. There is only so much we can do to heal and build resilience on a personal level—resilience is also dependent on the structures around us, at the interpersonal, organizational, community, and policy levels. We shape these systems, but these systems also shape us.

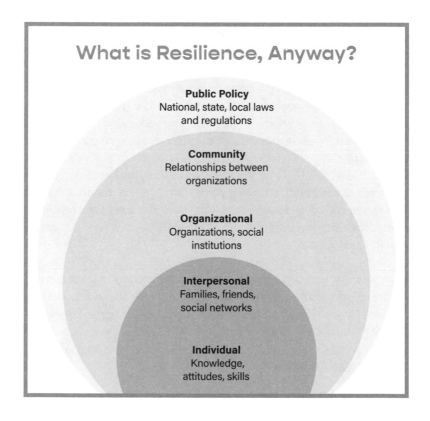

What is Resilience, Anyway?

Public Policy
National, state, local laws
and regulations

Community
Relationships between
organizations

Organizational
Organizations, social
institutions

Interpersonal
Families, friends,
social networks

Individual
Knowledge,
attitudes, skills

Imagine a world where if we experienced harassment, the responsibility wasn't just on us to heal—but there were structures around us to support us?

What if we created new rituals or ceremonies for our friends to participate in when we experience harassment, just like meal trains for new parents, winter solstice bonfires to bring light into the darkness, or gathering to hold the grief that comes with the loss of a loved one?

What if corporations and organizations were restructured to include more time off, self-care budgets, or collective trauma and healing funds to respond to harassment?

What if we created community structures where everyone was trained in bystander intervention, and where restorative justice processes could be accessed for free when harassment occurred?

And what if we demanded policy solutions like mandatory trainings that addressed all forms of harassment and discrimination (not just sexual harassment), or universal health care that included free therapy, or initiatives to get bystander intervention into schools?

Resilience cannot exist in the realm of the individual alone. The solution is not just self-soothing bubble baths, lattes, and chocolates. It can't even just be long heart-to-hearts with our friends about what happened, or brilliantly led healing meditations. Those things can be (and are!) part of the solution, but not the whole solution. In the words of Wade, "You have to do it on your own, but you can't do it alone."

We need to work toward building resilience into every facet of our society, and at the same time we need to get real about the world we're living in. Currently, few of us have these supports in place. The only thing we have full control over is us. In this next section, we'll walk through some personal practices for healing from harassment.

PERSONAL PRACTICES FOR HEALING FROM HARASSMENT

The first step toward addressing the trauma of harassment is to feel every single emotion it brings up for you. Like, really feel it. Pain, exhaustion, frustration, anger, rage, disappointment, resignation . . . these emotions are all completely normal.

This is easier said than done. While these emotions may be normal, they are anything but comfortable. Therapy and coaching can be effective, but they are often cost-prohibitive.

We've sketched out a three-part process with activities designed to help you metabolize and heal from your experience of having been harassed or having witnessed it. Each part of the process has three subcomponents. Our goal is to give you a tried-and-true road map to support your healing.

1. We start with a grounding activity, like a breathing exercise or brief meditation, to help you fully arrive and be in the present moment so you can take on what's next from a place of strength, resilience, and stability.

2. Next is a processing activity. Here, we want you to turn toward and face what happened by writing down part of your story and how you understand it. If at any point you need to stop the processing activity, that's okay! Listen to what your body needs. Breathe.

3. The final activity is designed to help you "metabolize" or "integrate" what happened by moving your body and remembering who you are, and why you're awesome. We want to help you make sure the pain doesn't get stuck in your body, and to do that we offer this activity as a way for it to run through your body.

If the recommended flows below don't resonate with you, feel free to mix and match to make something that works for you.

STEP 1: Getting Your Story Out

By writing down your story of harassment, you start to "externalize" it, or bring it outside of your body and into the world. Research by Jill Dimond, Ph.D. has shown that when people have shared their stories on RightToBe.

org alongside the stories of over 18,000 others, it has helped them to understand that even though harassment is something that happened to them, it wasn't about them. It was a result of the messed-up, prejudiced world that we live in. That simple framework shift has helped make them more likely to take action addressing harassment—for example, action as simple but profound as sharing their story with their dad.[79]

- **Grounding activity:** Box Breathing. How we breathe communicates to our brain how we're feeling.[80] Quick and shallow breathing makes our brain think we're stressed out, and it starts to send stress signals across our body. When we intentionally slow our breathing, our brain gets the message that we are safe and it's time to relax. In short, we can metagame our brains to shift toward feeling how we want to feel: neat! One way to slow your breathing intentionally is called "box breathing." You do it on a count of four:

  o Inhale: one, two, three, four . . .

  o Pause: one, two, three, four. . . .

  o Exhale: one, two, three, four . . .

  o Pause: one two, three, four . . .

  o Repeat as needed.

- **Processing activity:** Write down your story of harassment. What happened? How did it make you feel? Write it down—it doesn't need to be eloquent or beautiful, it just needs to be your truth. You can share it anonymously on RightToBe.org if that feels comfortable. When you're done, stare at it for a few seconds and take a deep breath in and a long, slow breath out. Well done.

- **Metabolizing activity:** Shake it out. After going through the process of reliving and writing your story, it's helpful to build resilience by moving some of those tough emotions through you. Think of eating as a metaphor: you chewed it up, let it move through you, and now it's time to flush it and get on with your day. Some people like to flush things through with upregulating activities (like dancing, running, jumping), while others prefer down regulating activities (like journaling, breathing, or yoga). You can also pick depending on your mood. Here's an upregulating exercise called "Shake it Out." It was taught to Emily at a retreat she attended, and it goes like this:

Your Story

_____

_____

_____

_____

_____

_____

_____

_____

_____

_____

_____

_____

_____

_____

_____

_____

_____

_____

_____

_____

o   Start with your right hand, shake it five times while you count out loud.

o   Go to your left hand, shake it five times while you count out loud.

o   Go to your right foot, shake it five times while you count out loud.

o   Go to your left foot, shake it five times while you count out loud.

o   Now, go back to your right hand, and this time, count only to four. Move through your other three limbs, also only counting to four.

o   Repeat by counting to three while shaking each limb.

o   Repeat by counting to two while shaking each limb.

o   Repeat by counting to one while shaking each limb.

By now, you should feel a little tired, and *very* proud of yourself.

STEP 2: Getting Really Mad

Harassment creates new wounds but can also reopen old ones. This next processing activity is inspired by Sarno's *The Mindbody Prescription* and is an iteration of how he tells his patients to address long-term unexplained pain.

- **Grounding activity:** Do a body scan. Notice where you feel places of holding, tension, sensation, or lack thereof? When you feel your body as a whole, where does it hurt? Your heart? Your gut? Your head? Somewhere else?

- **Processing activity:** Spend fifteen minutes making a list of what you're angry about. Make a list of *everything* you're angry about: the harassment, your home life, your work life, politics, the world—get it all out. Write until nothing else comes out of you. If you have time left over, spend that time holding this list and looking at it while concentrating on your breath.

- **Metabolizing activity:** Write yourself a meditation. For example, "I am strong," or "I've got me," or "I am resilient." Count how many things you were angry about. Then, write down your meditation on another piece of paper that many times. When you're done, put both pieces of paper in front of you. Let your anger be just as true as the light you bring into this world.

You certainly didn't ask to be harassed. And to be clear, none of that is your fault. But the science of resilience reminds us that how we tell our story matters deeply. It matters so much, in fact, that it shapes our future story.

When you're experiencing a lot of traumatic events, it's easy to see other things—or even everything—as trauma. It's harder to see joy, gratitude, and beauty in times where our minds are clouded. But finding meaning in the middle of traumatic events is what resilient people do.[81]

This next activity is about letting our pain and our resilience coexist.

- **Grounding activity:** Sit in a chair. Feel your feet flat on the floor. Feel your butt in the seat; feel your back on the chair. Quiet the distractions around you. Take a deep breath and exhale.

- **Processing activity:** Work on making sense of what happened to you. There will be lingering negative emotions surrounding your experience for a long time. On one side of a paper, identify those emotions without judgement. Just let them be. On the other side of your paper, identify what, if anything, this moment brought to you. Were you reminded that there are folks in your life who care? Did you learn something about yourself? Are you celebrating that you took care of yourself? List those things, too, and let them be. All of this is true. Notice how it feels to sit in a messy narrative—do you find yourself wanting to frame this moment as either "just good" or "just bad"? If so, find your butt in your seat and your back on the chair again, and see what it feels like to let it be exactly what it is.

- **Metabolizing activity:** Shout/dance it out. Pick a favorite song that makes you feel like the strong, amazing, confident, and resilient human that you are. Turn it up, shut the door, and sing it at the top of your lungs. Not a singer? Dance it out. Let your body express itself however it needs to. In the words of poet Mary Oliver, "You only have to let the soft animal of your body love what it loves."[82]

Here are a few additional tips to build resilience. Keep them in your back pocket:

- Share your story with a friend, family member, or partner. Having a supportive community around you is critical to resilience.

- Make a playlist to boost you when you get knocked off balance by life.

- Keep a list of things that help you when you're not feeling your best. Maybe it's meditation, exercise, calling a friend, writing, a hug, or something else. Turn back to this list when you need it. Add to this list as you learn more about yourself and what you need.

- Discuss with others how they build their own resilience. Add those methods to your list. Try them out and see how they feel.

- Perform an energy audit. Take a moment to think about all the things that give you energy, and that make you excited. Then, in contrast, think about all the things that take energy away from you and leave you feeling depleted. You can't avoid all the things that make you feel depleted, but what we've found is that awareness leads to choice. Use your awareness of what makes you feel depleted to make different choices. Can you approach certain activities differently? Can you take care of yourself differently?

CHOOSE HEALING

We are rarely only bystanders. We are oftentimes people who have been harmed, and people who have harmed. But no matter which shoes we're standing in at any given moment, we deserve care and healing.

Viktor Frankl, an Austrian neurologist and psychologist who survived the Holocaust, writes, "Everything can be taken from a [person] but one thing: the last of the human freedoms—to choose one's attitude in any given set of circumstances, to choose one's own way."

Healing our trauma is a profound choice we can all make for ourselves. It's also a profound gift we can give each other, our society, and generations to come.

We owe it to ourselves and our world to choose healing.

BYSTANDER INTERVENTION AS A WAY OF LIFE

Now it's time to put together everything we've learned. The next time you see harassment:

- Assess the situation and your safety,

- Identify what is holding you back from intervening, hold those concerns as true, and

- Decide if one (or more) of the 5Ds works for you.

Bystander intervention takes courage, but its effect is tangible. It shows people who are experiencing harassment that they aren't alone, and that what happened to them isn't okay. It's a step closer to a world free from harassment.

INTO YOUR POWER, BEYOND THE 5DS
To intervene, first remember you have power in moments of harassment.

Surely, the goal of ending harassment can feel hopeless because the root causes are big: racism, sexism, homophobia, ableism, xenophobia, transphobia, sizeism, colorism, and hate of all forms. These become entrenched into systems, laws, policies, and procedures—and they can feel immovable.

But just because they feel immovable, it doesn't mean they are.

In organizing work, we often say "work where you're rooted," a figurative flourish that enjoins us to engage in the work physically near us. When you witness harassment, you have the opportunity to directly change culture by modeling a new way to show up.

The 5Ds are an invitation to notice our power. Noticing our power lets us choose action. Our actions help us heal. Our healing enables cycles of healing and incites transformation within ourselves and our communities.

Here at Right To Be, we talk a lot to people who, just like you and me, are trying to end harassment—people leading massive companies, writing public policy, or telling stories and building tools that shape our lives. So many of them are working to bring bystander intervention to scale in their organizations, streets, and corners of the internet.

"Systems just aren't made of bricks they're mostly made of people"

—CRASS, an English art collective and punk rock band formed in Epping, Essex, in 1977

We hold it as true that most corporations and policymakers are at the helm of upholding harassment culture. We also hold it as true that many of the people trying to repair these systems from the inside out are thoughtful, pragmatic-yet-hopeful, and values-aligned—and many of them have been harmed by these systems themselves and joined in hopes of improving them.

Just as we sat with our own messy narratives in the last chapter, we also have to learn how to sit in the messy narrative of the world we live in. In that messy narrative, we find many people who have harmed and been harmed, but who are committed to doing better, repairing, and getting it right.

You are one of those people.

Now, it's time to extend bystander intervention—and your power to change our world through small, meaningful actions—even further.

When we do the small, sometimes uncomfortable acts of setting boundaries, saying "no," moving and nourishing our bodies, caring for our mental and emotional health, and/or asking for what we need and deserve, we heal and grow. When we take care of ourselves, we "power up" to take care of those around us.

When we refuse to speak on an all-white or all-male panel, advocate for better parental leave policies for all genders, or push companies to commit to equity in the hiring process—that, too, is bystander intervention.

And when we share our knowledge about caring for others, intervene on their behalf, or intervene on our own behalf, we pass along the wisdom and tools for the next person to stand beside us and create a better world, one small action after another.

It's going to be imperfect, and that's okay.

Bystander intervention doesn't always work out the way we want it to. Maybe you froze when you meant to take action. Maybe you planned to Delay but couldn't catch up with the person who was harassed. Maybe you intervened but can't tell if you did the right thing or not, or if your action was appreciated.

Doing the next right thing doesn't mean doing the next perfect thing.

We put lots of pressure on ourselves and others to be perfect. Perfectionism can show up as a symptom of white supremacist culture, according to Kenneth Jones and Tema Okun, authors of *Dismantling Racism: A*

We invite you to make a plan

What are the next three small actions I can take to intervene on behalf of myself?

1. _____

2. _____

3. _____

What are the next three small actions I can take to intervene on behalf of others—even when I'm not witnessing harassment?

1. _____

2. _____

3. _____

What are the next three small actions I can take to bring others on this journey with me—to equip them with tools to care for themselves and their communities?

1. _____

2. _____

3. _____

Workbook for Social Change Groups.[83] But the desire to "get it right" can also emerge from very real trauma for those of us who have borne the brunt of others' "getting it wrong" and causing harm in our lives.

We see you. We know the stakes feel high. But if we believe it has to be perfect or not at all, we make intervention impossible. In our real world, it's never perfect.

We've shared with you everything we know about bystander intervention, but it's up to you to make these tools your own. Things might get messy. You might second-guess yourself or recall your actions and wish you'd done something else instead. When you notice these thoughts, you can make the decision not to judge yourself. Instead, choose to learn and reflect with yourself and others. And most importantly, keep trying.

YOU'VE GOT THIS

Bystander intervention is about caring for the most vulnerable parts of ourselves and others. It's a salve designed to heal what hurts when the world wounds us.

Now it's yours.

We can't wait to see how you make this your own. People have practiced bystander intervention in many forms throughout history, but we're writing in a moment when people are especially hungry to take action and use these tools in their homes, workplaces, and communities.

We hope you'll take what's here, digest it, practice it, expand on it, and tell us about it. Our most sincere dream is that together, we'll all push the boundaries of what's possible by taking small, meaningful actions to care for each other—so much so as to render this book outdated.

As you go into the world to practice the 5Ds, know that we, and the many who've come before us, are standing by your side. You're not alone—and if you remember only one thing from this book, let it be this:

We've got your back.

Resources

This appendix contains resources and organizations to support you as you seek to implement bystander intervention into your life.

Answer Key to Superpower Quiz in Chapter 4:

If you answered . . .

- mostly A: your Superpower is DIRECT

- mostly B: your Superpower is DOCUMENT

- mostly C: your Superpower is DELAY

- mostly D: your Superpower is DISTRACT

- mostly E: your Superpower is DELEGATE

Some books that inspire us:

- *Conflict Is Not Abuse: Overstating Harm, Community Responsibility, and the Duty of Repair* by Sarah Schulman

- *Emergent Strategy: Shaping Change, Changing Worlds* by adrienne maree brown

- *My Grandmother's Hands: Racialized Trauma and the Pathway to Mending Our Hearts and Bodies* by Resmaa Menakem, MSW LICSW SEP

- *So You Want to Talk About Race* by Ijeoma Oluo

- *The Black Friend: On Being a Better White Person* by Frederick Joseph

- *The Mindbody Prescription: Healing the Body, Healing the Pain* by John E. Sarno, M.D.

- *What Happened to You?: Conversations on Trauma, Resilience, and Healing* by Oprah Winfrey and Bruce D. Perry

Podcasts that inspire us:

- *Politically Re-Active* by W. Kamau Bell and Hari Kondabolu

- *Super Soul* by Oprah Winfrey

Organizations that inspire us:

- Asian Americans Advancing Justice (AAJC)

- Color of Change

- Emergent Strategy Ideation Institute (ESII)

- Eye to Eye

- Girls for Gender Equity (GGE)

- GLSEN

- International Women's Media Foundation (IWMF)

- #MeToo

- National Center for Transgender Equality (NCTE)

- National Women's Law Center (NWLC)

- NYC Anti-Violence Project (AVP)

- PEN America

- Presencing Institute

- Southern Poverty Law Center (SPLC)

- Transgender Law Center (TLC)

Digital Security Reading:

- For more information on tightening your own digital security, check out this digital safety kit at: https://iheartmob.org/pages/digital-safety-kit

About the Authors

JORGE ARTEAGA's passion for history, places, and people, combined with his ability to plan and execute, have allowed him to bring his operational skills to serve in the social justice movement. His background in operations and in serving marginalized communities has informed his holistic approach to creating processes and systems that consider every aspect of a person's experience. Jorge has worked on racial justice, LGBTQ+, and arts education initiatives along the East Coast. He hopes to continue contributing to the social justice movement by ensuring all the phenomenal people leading the movement have the tools and resources required to enact real-world changes. Jorge earned his BA in American Studies from SUNY College at Old Westbury, his MA in American Studies at the City College of New York, and his MS in Project Management and Operations at Southern New Hampshire University.

EMILY MAY is an international leader in the movement to end harassment in all its forms. In 2005, at the age of twenty-four, she cofounded Right To Be in New York City, and in 2010, she became its first full-time executive director. Emily has won eleven awards for her work and been featured in over two hundred news media outlets, including *People* magazine, the *New York Times*, and NPR. Emily holds a bachelor's degree from New York University, a master's degree from the London School of Economics, and is a Prime Movers Fellow and an Ashoka Fellow. She lives in Brooklyn with her partner, Day, and their two beautiful kids, Ari and Olive.

Acknowledgments

This book is the culmination of hundreds of brilliant minds who have come through the doors of Right To Be since 2005—as volunteers, activists, staff, and board members. It would not be possible without the 18,000+ of you who shared your stories with us, or the 500,000+ who came to our trainings. We've learned so much from each and every one of you. This book is as much yours as it is ours.

Jorge wants to thank his mom, Miriam, for encouraging him and teaching him to stand up for what he believes in and to treat others with kindness and respect. He wants to thank his Aunt Carmen for living her life in service of supporting and uplifting her community. It is with their example that Jorge shows up to this work of creating a better world—because he saw what they were able to make possible. He also thanks his partner, Luis, who has been one of his biggest fans throughout this journey.

Emily also wants to thank her mom for teaching her that she could do anything (and for being exuberant about everything she actually pulled off), her dad for showing her how to dream big and work hard, and her stepmom for teaching her the gift of deep care (and showering her in it). She also wants to thank her kids, Ari and Olive—for pushing her to grow beyond what she ever thought was possible—and her partner, Day, for being endlessly supportive and down for the journey, backward and forward.

There are a few people who threw down to make this book happen. The first of them is Kate McKean, who asked us to write a book ten years ago. We weren't ready, but when we reached out again, she jumped in without hesitation. Thanks for believing in this book before we believed in it, Kate.

We also have to thank our editors, Zack Knoll and Samantha Weiner, and our coworkers Apurva Tandon and Malikia Brown, who have painstakingly gone through each and every word in this book to make sure it aligns with our vision and values. We also want to thank our wonderful team at ABRAMS: Diane Shaw, Glenn Ramirez, Rachael Marks, and Jennifer Brunn. Thank you to Daniel Fernandez, our fact-checker, who helped us make sure we are telling the stories in the book the way that the people who experienced them could stand behind and feel supported by.

Endnotes

1   As measured by anonymous polls at the end of our trainings, 2020-2021.

2   As measured by anonymous polls at the end of the training, 2020-2021.

3   #MomentofTruth, Tumblr, "The election is over, but its impact is not . . ." November 28, 2016, https://momentof truth2016.tumblr.com/.

4   Dr. Mishal Reja, ABC news, "Trump's 'Chinese Virus' tweet helped lead to rise in racist anti-Asian Twitter content: Study" March 18, 2021.

5   LaWanda Yanosik Holland in discussion with Emily May, 2017.

6   Tara Haelle, "Identity-first vs. Person-first Language Is an Important Distinction," *Covering Health*, July 31, 2019, https://health-journalism.org/blog/2019/07/identity-first-vs-person-first-language-is-an-important-distinction/.

7   adrienne maree brown, *Emergent Strategy: Shaping Change, Changing Worlds* (Chico: AK Press, 2017), 41.

8   Google ngram: https://books.google.com/ngrams/graph?content=catcalling&year_start=1800&year_end=2019&corpus=26&smoothing=3&direct_url=t1%3B%2Ccatcalling%3B%2Cc0.

9   Martin Luther King Jr., "Remaining Awake Through a Great Revolution" (speech, Oberlin College, June 1965), https://www2.oberlin.edu/external/EOG/BlackHistoryMonth/MLK/CommAddress.html.

10   *What I Hear When You Say*, "Viewing Guide: Race Card," accessed October 6, 2021, https://bento.cdn.pbs.org/hostedbento-prod/filer_public/whatihear/7-Race_Card-Viewing_Guide.pdf.

11   Kendra Cherry, "Heuristics and Cognitive Biases," verywellmind, April 11, 2021, https://www.verywellmind.com/what-is-a-heuristic-2795235.

12   *Short Wave*, "Understanding Unconscious Bias," produced by Rebecca Ramirez, aired July 15, 2020 on NPR, https://www.npr.org/2020/07/14/891140598/understanding-unconscious-bias.

13   Howard J. Ross, "3 Ways to Make Less Biased Decisions," *Harvard Business Review*, April 16, 2015, https://hbr.org/2015/04/3-ways-to-make-less-biased-decisions.

14   Sherry Gaba, "Understanding Fight, Flight, Freeze and the Fawn Response," *Psychology Today*, August 22, 2020, https://www.psychologytoday.com/us/

blog/addiction-and-recovery/202008/understanding-fight-flight-freeze-and-the-fawn-response.

15 Rommy von Bernhardi et al. "What Is Neural Plasticity?" *Advances in Experimental Medicine and Biology* 1015 (2017): 1-15. doi:10.1007/978-3-319-62817-2_1.

16 JR Thorpe, "How Neuroscience Could Help Address Racism," Bustle, September 20, 2016: https://www.bustle.com/articles/184790-can-you-unlearn-racism-by-re-training-your-brain.

17 Available online at https://implicit.harvard.edu/implicit/selectatest.html.

18 Nilanjana Dasgupta and Anthony Greenwald, "On the Malleability of Automatic Attitudes: Combating Automatic Prejudice with Images of Admired and Disliked Individuals," *Journal of Personality and Social Psychology* 81 (2001): 800–814.

19 "Fatal Violence Against the Transgender and Gender Non-Conforming Community in 2021," Human Rights Campaign, accessed October 5, 2021, https://www.hrc.org/resources/fatal-violence-against-the-transgender-and-gender-non-conforming-community-in-2021.

20 For a brief explainer, see: "Gay Hanky Codes," accessed October 5, 2021, https://user.xmission.com/~trevin/hanky.html and https://www.refinery29.com/en-us/2018/05/200229/lgbtq-secret-handkerchief-code-language.

21 Jackie Bischof, "If You're a Woman, 'Safety Work' Is a Part of Your Daily Existence," Quartz, October 24, 2018, https://qz.com/1433494/all-the-things-women-do-to-avoid-sexual-harassment/.

22 Patrick Worrall, "Do Black Americans Commit More Crime?" *Channel 4 News*, November 27, 2014, https://www.channel4.com/news/factcheck/factcheck-black-americans-commit-crime.

23 German Lopez, "Confronting the Myth that 'Black Culture' is Responsible for Violent Crime in America," Vox, September 1, 2016, https://www.vox.com/2016/9/1/11805346/violent-crime-america-barry-latzer-book-review.

24 Karen Nitkin "Bullying, Microaggression, and Other Terms" Hopkins Medicine (January 28, 2020): https://www.hopkinsmedicine.org/news/articles/bullying-microaggression-and-other-terms.

25 Chelsea Willness, Piers Steel, and Kibeom Lee, "A Meta-Analysis of the Antecedents and Consequences of Workplace Sexual Harassment," *Personnel Psychology*, February 2007, https://onlinelibrary.wiley.com/doi/10.1111/j.1744-6570.2007.00067.x. See also: https://www.weps.org/sites/default/files/2020-12/WEPs_GUIDANCE_Sexual_Harassment.pdf.

26 "Who Is Protected from Employment Discrimination?" U.S. Equal Employment Opportunity Commission, accessed October 7, 2021, https://www.eeoc.gov/employers/small-business/3-who-protected-employment-discrimination.

27 "Harassment," U.S. Equal Employment Opportunity Commission, accessed October 7, 2021, https://www.eeoc.gov/harassment.

28 "Title VII of the Civil Rights Act of 1964," U.S. Equal Employment Opportunity Commission, accessed October 5, 2021, https://www.eeoc.gov/statutes/title-vii-civil-rights-act-1964#.

29 "Sexual Harassment," U.S. Equal Employment Opportunity Commission, accessed October 7, 2021, https://www.eeoc.gov/sexual-harassment.

30 According to a 2015 study by Cornell University and Right To Be

31 PKC, Twitter message to Right To Be, September 30, 2021.

32 "The Social-Ecological Model: A Framework for Prevention," Centers

for Disease Control and Prevention, accessed October 10, 2021, https://www.cdc.gov/violenceprevention/about/social-ecologicalmodel.html.

33 "Facts about Retaliation," EEOC (October 10, 2021): https://www.eeoc.gov/facts-about-retaliation.

34 For further background, see Roy L. Brooks, "Use of Civil Rights Act of 1866," *Cornell Law Review*, January 1977, https://scholarship.law.cornell.edu/cgi/viewcontent.cgi?article=4101&context=clr.

35 "Jim Crow Museum of Racist Memorabilia," Ferris State University, accessed October 5, 2021, https://www.ferris.edu/HTMLS/news/jimcrow/. "Sex Stereotypes of African Americans Have Long History" NPR (May 7, 2007): https://www.npr.org/templates/story/story.php?storyId=10057104.

36 Janelle Griffith, "'They took my baby': Man killed by Texas police after intervening in dispute, family says," NBC News, October 5, 2020, https://www.nbcnews.com/news/us-news/they-took-my-baby-man-killed-texas-police-after-intervening-n1242132.

37 Will Carless and Michael Corey, "To Protect and Slur," Reveal News, June 14, 2019, https://revealnews.org/article/inside-hate-groups-on-facebook-police-officers-trade-racist-memes-conspiracy-theories-and-islamophobia/.

38 Sam Biddle, "Police Surveilled George Floyd Protests With Help From Twitter-Affiliated Startup Dataminr," The Intercept, July 9, 2020, https://theintercept.com/2020/07/09/twitter-dataminr-police-spy-surveillance-black-lives-matter-protests/.

39 Perez, Maria. Newsweek. "Police Called on Black University of Massachusetts Amherst Employee While He Was Walking to Work." 18 September 2018.

40 See this analysis from the Projection on Government Oversight, for example: https://www.pogo.org/analysis/2019/03/caught-between-conscience-and-career/.

41 Miz Cracker, "Beware the Bachelorette! A Report from the Straight Lady Invasion of Gay Bars." Slate, August 13, 2015, https://slate.com/human-interest/2015/08/should-straight-women-go-to-gay-bars-a-drag-queen-reports-on-the-lady-invasion.html.

42 J. M. Darley and B. Latane, Bystander intervention in emergencies: Diffusion of responsibility, *Journal of Personality and Social Psychology*, 8(4, Pt.1), 1968, 377–383. https://doi.org/10.1037/h0025589. J. M. Darley and B. Latane, Group inhibition of bystander intervention in emergencies, *Journal of Personality and Social Psychology*, 10(3), 215–221. https://doi.org/10.1037/h0026570

43 Day, Bek. News.com.au. "Woman's Act Of Sisterhood At The Gym Goes Viral" 18 Feb 2018.

44 Workshop hosted by Right To Be, 2020.

45 https://stopstreetharassment.org/our-work/nationalstudy/2018-national-sexual-abuse-report/.

46 IPSOS, L'Oreal Paris, 2019 https://www.loreal.com/en/articles/commitments/l-oreal-paris-stands-up-against-street-harassment/.

47 Alexandra Samuels, "'It was so creepy': TikToker films himself saving teen from man at mall," The Daily Dot, February 6, 2021. https://www.dailydot.com/irl/tiktoker-saves-teen-girl-man-mall/.

48 For example, see Cassi Claytor, "Shopping while Black" *The Guardian*, June 24, 2019, https://www.theguardian.com/commentisfree/2019/jun/24/shopping-while-black-yes-bias-against-black-customers-is-real.

49 Interview conducted by Jorge Arteaga, 2021.

50 Read the full story online at https://www.ihollaback.org/blog/2019/07/31/

holla-go-noticed-man-age-35-45-walking-behind/.

51 "NYPD Rolls Out New De-escalation Tactics Training," Spectrum News, June 24, 2021, https://www.ny1.com/nyc/all-boroughs/news/2021/06/24/nypd-rolls-out-new-icat-de-escalation-tactics-training.

52 See the original exchange online at https://twitter.com/juliaioffe/status/725637201372020736 and https://twitter.com/juliaioffe/status/1117968251219263491.

53 Elle Hunt, "Milo Yiannopoulos, Rightwing Writer, Permanently Banned from Twitter," *The Guardian*, July 20, 2016.

54 Kurt Chirbas and Alexander Smith "#LoveforLeslieJ: Thousands Rally Behind 'Ghostbusters' Star Leslie Jones After Twitter Abuse," NBC News, July 19, 2016, https://www.nbcnews.com/pop-culture/movies/loveforlesliej-thousands-rally-behind-ghostbusters-star-leslie-jones-after-twitter-n612176.

55 There is considerable coverage of Thao's situation, but a good place to start is the *Washington Post*'s "How Street Harassment Became a National Conversation," online at https://www.washingtonpost.com/blogs/she-the-people/wp/2015/01/02/how-street-harassment-became-a-national-conversation-in-2014/. Gothamist also covered the case: https://gothamist.com/news/more-allegations-towards-supposed-subway-pervert.

56 WITNESS has a fabulous range of resources online. You can see a summary of them at: https://www.witness.org/resources/.

57 For example, in Texas. See https://www.sos.state.tx.us/elections/laws/advisory2018-11.shtml.

58 Sarah Maslin Nir, "How 2 Lives Collided in Central Park, Rattling the Nation," *New York Times*, June 14, 2020, https://www.nytimes.com/2020/06/14/nyregion/central-park-amy-cooper-christian-racism.html.

59 Michael Tram, "Explainer: Video Dominates Trial in George Floyd's Death," Associated Press March 31, 2021, https://apnews.com/article/video-dominates-derek-chauvin-trial-explained-f7608641d2fdbd6a8443691fd7ca1625.

60 Nicholas Bogel-Burroughs, "An Outspoken Off-Duty Firefighter Testified," *New York Times*, March 30, 2021, https://www.nytimes.com/2021/03/30/us/genevieve-hansen-testimoy.html.

61 "What George Floyd Changed," Politico Magazine, May 23, 2021, https://www.politico.com/news/magazine/2021/05/23/what-george-floyd-changed-490199.

62 "Austin Park Ranger Pushed into Water After Reportedly Warning Group About Social Distancing," Fox 7 Austin News, May 1, 2020, https://www.fox7austin.com/news/austin-park-ranger-pushed-into-water-after-reportedly-warning-group-about-social-distancing.

63 Josh Rivera, "Woman Spits on 7-Eleven Counter After Being Asked to Wear a Mask," *USA Today*, July 2, 2020, https://www.usatoday.com/story/money/2020/07/02/7-eleven-mask-incident-viral-video-spits-counter/5368869002/.

64 Charlotte Klein, "'I'm afraid to open Twitter,'" *Vanity Fair*, March 26, 2021, https://www.vanityfair.com/news/2021/03/harassment-of-female-journalists-is-putting-news-outlets-to-the-test.

65 Read the story online at: https://nyc.ihollaback.org/2016/01/15/being-a-badass-bystander-on-the-4-train/?preview=true.

66 Read the story at: https://www.ihollaback.org/blog/2021/05/13/public-harassment-i-was-stand-ing-the-appropriate/.

67 Read the full story online at https:// www.ihollaback.org/blog/2016/04/13/ are-you-okay/.

68 Mark Berman, "What the Police Officer Who Shot Philando Castile Said About the Shooting," *Washington Post*, June 21, 2017, https://www.washingtonpost.com/ news/post-nation/wp/2017/06/21/what-the-police-officer-who-shot-philando-castile-said-about-the-shooting/.

69 Katie Rogers, "Mark Zuckerberg Covers His Laptop Camera. You Should Consider It, Too," June 22, 2016, https:// www.nytimes.com/2016/06/23/ technology/personaltech/mark-zuckerberg-covers-his-laptop-camera-you-should-consider-it-too.html.

70 Learn more about Emily and her organization at https://www.unslutproject. com/.

71 Read the exchange here: https:// twitter.com/ChlooCondon/ status/1083874972009783301.

72 Jordan Moreau, "*New York Times* Defends Reporter," *Variety*, March 10, 2021, https://variety.com/2021/digital/ news/tucker-carlson-taylor-lorenz-new-york-times-harassment-1234927645/. For the clip, see Sara Pearl, Twitter, March 9, 2021, https://twitter.com/skenigsberg/ status/1369464714040840199?s=20.

73 Ted Johnson, "*New York Times* Calls Out Tucker Carlson for 'Calculated and Cruel' Segment Attacking Reporter," Deadline, March 10, 2021, https://deadline. com/2021/03/new-york-times-tucker-carlson-taylor-lorenz-1234711793/. See also: https://twitter.com/NYTimesPR/ status/1369747504565256193/photo/1.

74 Gregory Janson and Richard Hazler, "Brief Report: Trauma Reactions of Bystanders and Victims to Repetitive Abuse Experiences," *Violence and Victims* 19, no. 2 (May 2004): 239–55, 10.1891/088667004780927981.

75 Vilayanur Ramachandran, "The Neurons That Shaped Civilization," filmed 2009, TED video, 7:27, https://www.ted.com/ talks/vilayanur_ramachandran_the _neurons_that_shaped_civilization ?language=en.

76 Alan Woodruff, "What Is a Neuron?" *Queensland Brain Institute*, accessed October 6, 2021, https://qbi.uq.edu.au/ brain/brain-anatomy/what-neuron.

77 Resmaa Menakem, *My Grandmother's Hands: Racialized Trauma and the Pathway to Mending our Hearts and Bodies* (Las Vegas: Central Recovery Press, 2017).

78 Madeline Wade in discussion with Emily May, September 2021.

79 Dimond, Jill P., Michaelanne Dye, Daphne LaRose, Amy S. Bruckman, "Right To Be: The Role of Collective Storytelling in a Movement Building Organization." School of Interactive Computing, GVU, Georgia Institute of Technology. http://www.tandem.gatech. edu/wp-content/uploads/2016/10/story-telling-cscwRev2-final.pdf.

80 B Grace Bullock, "What Focusing on the Breath Does to Your Brain," *Greater Good Magazine*, October 31, 2019, https:// greatergood.berkeley.edu/article/item/ what_focusing_on_the_breath_does_to_ your_brain.

81 Jessica Stillman, "To Be More Resilient in a Crisis, Focus on Meaning, Not Happiness," *Inc.*, April 22, 2020, https:// www.inc.com/jessica-stillman/ to-be-more-resilient-in-a-crisis-focus-on-meaning-not-happiness.html.

82 Mary Oliver, "Wild Geese," in *Dream Work* (New York: Atlantic Monthly Press, 1986), 14.

83 Kenneth Jones and Tema Okun, *Dismantling Racism: A Workbook for Social Change Groups* (Durham: change-work, 2001).

Notes

Editor: Zack Knoll
Designer: Diane Shaw
Managing Editor: Glenn Ramirez
Production Manager: Rachael Marks

Library of Congress Control Number: 2021946854

ISBN: 978-1-4197-6216-1
eISBN: 978-1-64700-683-9

Text copyright © 2022 Right To Be, Jorge Arteaga, Emily May
Illustrations copyright © 2022 Lucila Perini

Cover © 2022 Abrams

Printed and bound in the United States
10 9 8 7 6 5 4 3 2 1

The material in this book is presented for informational purposes only and is not
a substitute for legal advice. Readers are advised to consult with an attorney if
they need legal advice on issues discussed in this book.

Abrams Image books are available at special discounts when purchased in
quantity for premiums and promotions as well as fundraising or educational
use. Special editions can also be created to specification. For details, contact
specialsales@abramsbooks.com or the address below.

Abrams Image® is a registered trademark of Harry N. Abrams, Inc.

ABRAMS The Art of Books
195 Broadway, New York, NY 10007
abramsbooks.com